African Folklore in the New World

African Folklore
in the New World

Edited by Daniel J. Crowley

University of Texas Press, Austin & London

International Standard Book Number 0-292-70326-0 (cloth);

0-292-70327-9 (paper)

Library of Congress Catalog Card Number 76-050962

The preface and the first five essays in this volume were

previously published in *Research in African Literatures* 7,

no. 2 (Fall 1976). The last essay will be published in

Research in African Literatures 8, no. 2 (Fall 1977).

CONTENTS

Preface   vii
Daniel J. Crowley

Ọba's Ear: A Yoruba Myth in Cuba and Brazil   3
William Bascom

Puttin' Down Ole Massa: African Satire in the New World   20
William D. Piersen

African and Afro-American Tales   35
Alan Dundes

"The Rarest Thing in the World":
Indo-European or African?   54
Steven S. Jones

After the Myth: Studying Afro-American
Cultural Patterns in the Plantation Literature   65
John F. Szwed and Roger D. Abrahams

The African Connection: Comments on
African Folklore in the New World   87
Richard M. Dorson

Notes on the Contributors   93

Index   95

PREFACE

Daniel J. Crowley

This collection of essays is dedicated to one side of an ongoing controversy and as such is a frank appeal to scholars of African literatures, oral and written, for understanding and support. Three of the papers presented here were read at the San Francisco meetings of the African Studies Association in October, 1975, dedicated to "African-American Interchange," where their significance was noted by a regrettably small audience. The fourth paper reports on a detailed study carried out in connection with the research of the other participants, and the fifth takes a fresh revisionistic look at African contributions, technical as well as artistic, to the development of New World cultures. Together they are the latest riposte of the Africanist folklorists in their long duel with the European Diffusionists over the origins of the tales told in the New World by Black people. As such, they answer the distinguished historical folklorist Richard Dorson's "African and Afro-American Folklore: A Reply to Bascom and Other Misguided Critics" (*Journal of American Folklore*, 88 [1975], 151–64), who is also given the final word in which to state his reactions to these essays. In spite of the specialized nature of the argument and the infinite complexities of the Type and Motif Indexes, the issues are so crucial both for Africans and for Afro-Americans that they warrant full presentation here.

In short, Dorson's contention is that, of the hundreds of tales he has collected from Black Americans, a mere 10 percent are of African origin. The dean of Africanist folklorists, William Bascom, here documents sixteen examples of a specifically Yoruba religious myth which have been collected in Brazil and Cuba, demonstrating not only that African narratives more complex and culture-bound than folktales could and did cross the Atlantic, but also that they have persisted with little modification in new and very different cultural milieux. In a parallel paper, Piersen describes the similar peregrinations of a characteristically African type of allusive song, validating at the same time the worth of old travel books normally disdained by document-oriented historiographers. Dundes sets out to answer Dorson's charges specifically, and manages not only to clarify the argument but also to make a number of telling revelations of African and probably-African tales in Dorson's own collections using his own methods. The paper by Steven Jones, although a veritable "forest of symbols" to the uninitiated, documents exactly how a once-"European" tale has been shown to be much more likely of African origin, and the joint effort of Szwed and Abrahams adds historical depth to the controversy.

At the recent Conference on African Oral Literature sponsored by the African Studies Center, University of California at Los Angeles (February 18–20, 1976), the African participants chose in their deliberations to ignore fictive narrative in favor of historical memorats, praise poetry, and epic literature. When this omission was pointed out, their reaction implied that storytelling was trivial and unimportant in comparison to these historical and pseudohistorical materials increasingly becoming more available for study. Yet, unlike most of these epics, fictional tales are truly Pan-African, and represent by far the longest tradition of collection and study in all of African Studies, beginning in 1828 with the publication of *Fables Sénégalaises recueillies de l'Oulof* (Paris: Nepvue, Firmin Didot, Ponthieu, 1828), a collection of Wolof animal tales translated into French verse by leBon Roger, the ex-Commandant of Senegal. One must also protest the fashion of deploring, in Lloyd W. Brown's words, "the negligible attention to African oral literature as literary art and . . . its usual role as grist for the statistical mills of the folklorist" (*RAL*, 6 [1975], 75). Recent American folklore research on Africa has been as "performance-oriented" as on all other areas, as witness Dan Ben-Amos's *Sweet Words: Storytelling Events in Benin* (Philadelphia: Institute for the Study of Human Issues, 1975), and as for statistics, where are they? Would that we had even a few!

As African scholars more and more shoulder the responsibility of exegesis and criticism of their unfamiliar forms and seemingly verbose styles, in attempting to bridge the chasms that separate verbal expression in different unrelated languages, we non-African scholars who do not control an African language automatically assign ourselves the non-evaluative chores, and we find that those so-called statistical mills, the Type and Motif Indexes, have ground out precious little of any value to us. In use for most of a century in every major folklore study and archive on earth, these Indexes are invaluable bibliographic aids to the comparative study of narrative which cannot be ignored or discarded. However, since their obvious European bias was admitted by their most recent compiler, the late Stith Thompson, and because African collections are only minimally represented, they provide more confusion than enlightenment on the patterns of distribution of particular tales across

Africa and the New World. "Types" are whole tales that travel through time and space as units, and all versions of any one Type are (sometimes) assumed to have had a common origin. "Motifs" are characters, objects, and incidents that recur in traditional narrative, but which can be repeatedly reinvented. Until the worldwide distribution patterns of these elements are known, we can only guess what they will reveal about the nature of storytelling, its vehicles of transmission, and its meanings and functions in human cultures—the major research goals of our discipline.

Rivaling the Hope-Crosby exchanges on prewar radio, this African/ Afro-American tale origin controversy has raged, if that is the *mot juste*, for nearly a quarter of a century since Dorson and I were studying with Herskovits and Bascom. Dundes and Piersen later studied with Dorson, while Jones is currently working with Dundes and me, so all civility and decorum have been maintained while degrees were earned and tenure granted. With extensive Caribbean and urban American field experience, Szwed and Abrahams have earned enviable reputations as academic boat-rockers. Essentially at issue is the trustworthiness of the Type and Motif Indexes, and by extension the disciplinary interests and methods of anthropologists and Black scholars as against European and Euro-American historians and literary scholars. Although it is unclear whether Dorson realizes it or not, we Africanists do not claim that *all* stories told by Blacks in the New World are African. Far from it! Considering the drastic experiences of enslavement and transportation plus centuries of massive multiple acculturation, it would be miraculous if the whole repertory had been preserved and no new items added. We merely claim that a much higher percentage than 10 percent of the tales are African, but as Dorson tellingly points out, he has the evidence and we do not, because no adequate Type and Motif Indexes exist for Africa or for Black America. We counter by charging that his basic reference sources are so misleading as to be worse than useless.

And thereby hangs a tale: in 1973, while conducting field research in Trinidad, I was invited to contribute a paper to a Festschrift honoring Dorson on his sixtieth birthday to be published in 1976 as *Folklore Today*. Thinking to make a conciliatory gesture suitable to the occasion, I chose a well-told local text of a tale I had never before encountered in the southern Caribbean, and which according to the Type Index was reported from Europe, Spanish America, and the Cape Verde Islands but not from Africa. After all, I am willing to concede that Black Trinidadians do indeed occasionally tell non-African tales, and the burden of the paper was to analyze the way the foreign tale had been localized into Trinidadian culture. Imagine my surprise two years later when Jones, starting with my text but bypassing the Type Index, turned up a number of African versions and then through Dundes learned of Bascom's then-unpublished treasure trove. My chagrin at missing the now-obvious clues changed to ill-concealed delight at the accidentally made point for our side, and then profound embarrassment that this particular piece will appear in Dorson's very Festschrift. It wasn't a plant, Dick, honest!

Although not directly concerned with the problems of research in the Black New World, readers of this volume cannot but find this controversy of some considerable interest, if for no other reason than its political overtones. The contributors join me in thanking the editors of *RAL* for this opportunity to state our case so fully, and in urging African scholars and all others to help us in documenting the distribution of African tales through more adequate Indexes.

African Folklore in the New World

OBA'S EAR: A YORUBA MYTH IN CUBA AND BRAZIL

William Bascom

As my professor, the late Melville J. Herskovits, emphasized, Afro-American studies can shed light on Africa. The myth of Oba's ear is a case in point. The myth itself began with the Yoruba people in Nigeria, but my encounter with it began in Cuba.

This is not a folktale, told as fiction—not an Uncle Remus tale. It is a sacred Yoruba myth, told as fact, about a Yoruba goddess who is still worshipped in Cuba and Brazil. The principal points that I wish to make are that this Yoruba myth has survived in the Americas in readily recognizable form, and that it could only have originated among the Yoruba of West Africa.

Perhaps I should preface this article by stating that I have no intention of disparaging Yoruba religion. The Yoruba, French, Spanish, and Portuguese texts are available for anyone to see, and I have translated them as accurately as I can. The two final Yoruba texts, in particular, were tape-recorded and then transcribed and translated by Yoruba men, and they provoked gales of laughter from Yoruba listeners.

In Havana in 1947, Berta, my wife, first heard the Yoruba myth of how Oba cut off her own ear (Aarne-Thompson O). Oba was cooking yam porridge (*amalá*), the favorite food of her husband, Shango. She was stirring and stirring it, when Oshun came to her house. Oshun asked, "What are you cooking?" "Yam porridge for Shango." Oshun said, "It will please him more if it has one of your ears." So Oba cut off her ear and cooked it in the porridge. When Shango ate it, he got his real strength. Oba took off her kerchief and showed him that she had cut off her ear because she loved him so much. Shango got mad and left her. He went to live with Oshun, which is what Oshun wanted. This is why Oba covers her left ear with her hand when she dances.

Shango is a Yoruba God of Thunder, and the two women are goddesses of the River Oshun, which flows past Oshogbo, Nigeria, and the River Oba, which is a tributary of the River Oshun that flows past Ogbomosho. Oya, who appears in other versions of this myth, is goddess of the River Oya, which is the River Niger. In Yoruba belief, all three goddesses were wives of Shango.

In 1948 when we went together to Cuba, half a dozen informants told us this myth in fragmentary form. A composite of these accounts would go as follows. Shango was the lover of Oshun, but the husband of Ǫba, and Ǫya was trying to take him away from Ǫba. Shango did not like Ǫba's cooking, but Ǫya was a very good cook. She told Ǫba to cut off an ear and cook it with okra stew (*quimbombo*) for Shango. Ǫba did so in order to keep Shango at home, and she covered the wound so that Shango would not see that her ear was missing. But Shango saw the ear in his stew and was angry, and never wanted Ǫba again. She left in shame, and he took Ǫya as his wife.

Only two of the six informants mentioned who advised Ǫba to cut off her ear; both named Ǫya. In one of the versions, Ǫshun was said to be Shango's senior wife and Ǫba was his junior wife. A seventh informant told a quite different myth in which Ǫya cut off Ǫba's ear when the two women were fighting.

Two more complete versions from Cuba have been published by Lydia Cabrera.[1] Changó had three wives, Obba, Oshún, and Oyá. Obba was the first of the three wives—the senior wife, the legitimate wife, and the respected wife. Her jealousy and the perfidious advice of Oshún, according to some, or Oyá, according to others, condemned her to live apart from her husband, who held her in great esteem, but who stopped living with her in marriage because she gave him her ear to eat.

Obba hoped that Changó would be faithful. One day she complained to Oshún that he did not spend much time with her. Oshún asked, "Do you want Changó to remain quietly at home?" "How much I would like that!" "Well then, cut off an ear, make okra stew (*cararú*) with yam porridge (*amalá*) and your ear, and give it to Changó to eat. When he swallows it and has it inside of him, he will love you much more." And Obba cut off an ear, made okra stew, and called Changó.

Changó was with Oyá. "Do you hear? Obba is calling me. I am going." Upset, Oyá said, "She is your favorite!" "She is my wife, I respect her." Obba had set the table. "Eat." Obba had her head covered with a white kerchief. "What's the matter, Obba? Why aren't you eating?" "I have no appetite." "Why are you sad?" "I never see you."

Changó finished and left. He went to see Oshún who told him, "Is it possible that a man as elegant as you are is not ashamed to live with a woman with a physical defect?" "What woman?" "Obba." And all was revealed. Changó tore off the white cloth with which she had covered her head and saw that she was lacking an ear. "What have you done, Obba! I will not abandon you, you are my senior wife; but as you have mutilated yourself, I will not live in your house any more."

The narrative continues with an episode in which Obba is confused with Oyá, and ends with the following: when Obba dances, she dances holding her hands to her head, concealing her ears. Cabrera's second version follows.

When Yemayá (Yemoja, Shango's mother) was talking with Obba, she told her what a glutton Changó was, and the quantities of corn meal and okra stew that had to be cooked for him. They were married, but Changó abandoned her. He left and spent many days away from home. Chango didn't want anything but drumming (*batá*) and feasting. In one of his absences, Elegguá (Elegba, Eshu) told Obba to give a feast; he looked for Changó and took him to the drumming that Obba prepared.

Oyá went to look for him to take him from the feast, but Changó was having a good time; he showed Oyá the head of a ram, and she fled in fright. As a sacrifice, and to "tie" Changó to her, Obba cut off her ear and put it in the okra stew (*quimbombó*). But Changó saw the ear floating in the stew, and he left. Then Obatalá covered Obba's head with a white kerchief, which she never takes off. These two goddesses were enemies from then on. Obba, who adores Changó, has never pardoned Oyá, who was the one who advised her about the ear. She lives apart, hiding her missing ear. Very respected, she takes care of her husband's house (*ilé*). But the sweetheart, the official concubine of the God of Thunder, is as jealous as his wife, Obba.

A somewhat different Cuban version was published by Lachatañeré.[2] Oba was the legitimate wife of Shangó, in charge of domestic affairs. She accompanied him on all his military expeditions in order to take care of his diet, which consisted of *amala* (corn meal with *quimbombó* and ram meat). One day Shangó went to a war that lasted a very long time. It was the war that he had with Ogún. Oba, as usual, followed her husband with the provisions.

The war was prolonged and, when he had the opportunity, Shangó went to Oba to regain his strength with the *amala*. With surpassing care, Oba employed her culinary art to satisfy the immeasurable appetite of her husband. But the battle continued. It continued so long that provisions became scarce, and it was increasingly difficult for Oba to find the ingredients of *amala*. But Oba multiplied her efforts. She sharpened her wits, and Shangó was never lacking for *amala*. But the day came when her efforts were in vain. Her cleverness failed. Oba could not find any ram meat to add to the *amala*. But, being a woman of great strength, Oba did not yield to misfortune. This time the corn meal was bubbling in the pot without meat, and Oba had the strength to cut off her two ears and add them to the pot. Thus Oba, who was a very beautiful woman, ceased being beautiful, and her spirits failed. She locked herself in her room and cried. "Ah, I am a repugnant woman without ears. Ah, I am the wife who has stopped being beautiful." That same day Shangó arrived with an erection and claimed his wife. "Oba, I have won the war. Come and share the victory with your husband." Oba remained silent. Beside himself, Shangó demanded the immediate presence of his wife, but Oba remained silent. Furious, the warrior went to search for her and found her stretched on the floor; he tried to pick her up, and found that she was lacking both ears. "Ah, wife, without *etí* (ears), I do not love you any more," exclaimed Shangó, and he fled from the place. In a little while Oba recovered and ran through the plains howling, "Ah, I am a woman without ears. Ah, I am a woman who has stopped being beautiful." And she went into the woods, always with the same lament. Oba shed so many tears that she turned into a river.

In Brazil the myth of Ǫba's ear was first reported in 1937 by Edison Carneiro, but with Ǫba confused with Ǫya.[3] I have not been able to see this early account,[4] but, as Roger Bastide notes, the error is corrected in a subsequent publication.[5] Óbá does not have one ear. She was a wife of Xangô, less loved than the others, and she believed the words of the favorite wife, Yansã (Ǫya), who told her that she had to cut off her ear to win the affection of Xangô. In dancing she conceals her left ear with her copper shield, with leaves, or simply with her hand.

According to another Brazilian version published by Pierre Verger,[6] Shango had many wives, and he spent his days and nights with them in turn; but he especially loved Oshoun, who knew how to please him with her kindness and voluptuousness. Pretty and coquettish, she used all the weapons of a woman to keep a man. This was not without exciting the jealousy of her co-wives, and Oba, less favored, came one day to ask her what was the secret that assured her the favors of their husband, Shango. Oshoun explained that the way to a man's heart is his stomach, and that her secret was to serve him his favorite food. Not without malice, she added that as a good co-wife she would show Oba how to prepare a certain soup at which Shango marveled, and she invited her to return a few hours later.

Oba returned at the appointed time. Oshoun had tied a cloth around her head that concealed her ears, and she had cooked a soup in which two mushrooms were floating. Oshoun showed them to Oba, telling her that they were her ears, which she had cut off and put into the pot; she added that Shango would be enchanted with it. Soon Shango arrived, ate the soup, found it excellent, and went to bed with Oshoun. Some days later the time came for Oba to take care of Shango. She followed the advice of Oshoun, cut off an ear, and cooked it in a soup for Shango. He showed no pleasure in seeing Oba disfigured and covered with blood, and he found the dish that she served repugnant.

At that moment Oshoun appeared, having removed the cloth from her head; her ears were intact, and she began to mock Oba. Furious, Oba threw herself at her rival, and a battle ensued. Shango flew into a rage, shot fire from his mouth, and thundered at his wives, who fled in fright and turned themselves into the two rivers that bear their names today. One must never mention the name of Oba when crossing the River Oshoun, lest she drown you immediately. Similarly, one must not speak of Oshoun when crossing the River Oba. These two rivers flow into each other, and at their confluence the waters are extremely agitated and beat furiously against each other in remembrance of their past adventure.

A third Brazilian version has been published by Roger Bastide.[7] Xangô had three wives, Yansan (Oya), Oxun (Oshun), and Obá, but Oxun was the favorite wife and Obá the abandoned one. The unhappy goddess (*orixa*), not knowing how to win the affection of her husband, one day asked Oxun how she was able to share Xangô's bed so easily. Malicious Oxun told her that she had a medicine, and, concealing her head in a cloth so that Obá could not see her lie, she said that she had cut off her ear to cook it in Xangô's okra stew (*cararú*). By eating it, he had made an unending erotic alliance with her. Then Obá cut off her ear and cooked it in her husband's food; but Xangô had hardly taken a bite of his stew when he rejected it in disgust and had Obá called to learn what she had put in the dish to make it so bad. Obá came, disfigured and bleeding, all in tears. Xangô exploded in anger. He sent his third wife away, having become too ugly to arouse his desire. When Obá manifests herself in the *candomblés* of Bahia, which is only rarely, she covers her left ear with leaves, or she conceals her head under a colored cloth.

Cuban and Brazilian versions of the myth are cited briefly in Bascom.[8]

Not having heard this myth in Nigeria, I enquired about it when I returned there with Mrs. Bascom in 1950–51, before the versions of Cabrera, Verger, and Bastide had been published. As in Cuba and Brazil, there are apparently not many worshipers of Oba in Nigeria, but I did find three informants who knew the myth about her ear. A Shango (*Sàngó*) worshiper in the town of Mekọ said that Oya, Oshun, and Oba (*Oya, Oṣun*, and *Obà*) were the three wives of Shango. Oba was the one who cut off her ear to make stew when Oya told her to do so, and Shango drove her away.

A priest of Oba in Oyọ said that Oba, Oshun, and Oya were all wives of Shango. Oba was the senior wife, but Shango loved Oya, his junior wife, more than he loved Oba. Oya told Oba to cut off her ear and cook it in okra stew (*ọbẹ ilá*) so that Shango would love Oba as much as he loved her. Oba cut off part of her left ear, and when Shango found it in his stew he drove her away, saying that he would have nothing more to do with her. In possession Ǫba dances with her hand over her left ear, and he himself also dances in that fashion. The River Ǫba rises near the village of Igbǫn, where she was born and where she became a deity, but her principal place of worship is Ogbomǫshǫ.

At Ogbomǫshǫ the priest of Ǫba confirmed that Igbǫn, on the road to Ilorin (about ten miles from Ogbomǫshǫ), where Ǫba became a deity and turned into the River Ǫba, is near the river's source, and that since the wars of the last century Ogbomǫshǫ has been her principal place of worship. He said that Ǫba and Ǫya were wives of Shango, but Ǫba left him and married Ajagún at Igbǫn. One of Ǫba's praise names is "Ǫba, who owns (red) parrot tail feathers and who fights on the left side" (*Ǫba eleko a ja osi*). He confirmed that Ǫba covers one ear with her hand in possession, but he said that he did not know why; and when told the myth, he said that he did not know it.

As told by Ǫshun worshipers at Ilesha, it was Ǫshun who caused Ǫba to cut off her ear. Ǫba was the senior wife of Shango, and when Shango married Ǫshun, Ǫba did all the housework for her, as Yoruba women do for seven days to show respect for the new wife. Ǫba made the fire, cooked the food, swept the floor, and so on. One day Ǫba asked Ǫshun to do something, and Ǫshun answered that Ǫba could not ask her to do anything. One day Ǫba asked Ǫshun why Shango loved her more than herself. Ǫshun had put blood from a pigeon on her ear and had wrapped her head in a headtie. She told Ǫba that when she cooked bean stew (*gbẹgiri*) for Shango she cut off a piece of her ear and put it in the stew. So Ǫba cut a piece of her ear and put it in Shango's stew, and Shango saw it. Ǫba told him how his junior wife had said that he liked stew that way, but Shango drove Ǫba away. Ǫba and Ǫshun are still enemies, and if a person takes water from the River Ǫba and puts it into the River Ǫshun, they will meet great trouble.

A version recorded at Oshogbo, Nigeria, by Pierre Verger[9] says that Ṣango had three wives, Ǫya, Ǫṣun, and Ǫba. Ǫṣun made very good food for Ṣango, and he loved her very much. One day she played a bad trick on Ǫba, who always sought to obtain cooking secrets that would assure her Ṣango's love. Ǫṣun put a large flat mushroom in the shape of an ear in the soup for Ṣango, and he went into ecstasies over the excellence of the meal. Ǫba went to find Ǫṣun and found her with a kerchief tied over her head, concealing her ears; she asked what Ǫṣun had done to prepare such a good dish. Ǫṣun replied that she had cut off her ears and had put them in the soup. Desiring to enter into Ṣango's good graces, when her turn came to make the food, Ǫba cut off an ear and cooked it in the soup. Ṣango found the ear in his dish and cried,

"What is this? I can't eat that!" and flew into a rage. When Ọṣun removed the kerchief tied over her head and showed Ọba her two ears intact, Ọba was furious and started to beat her. Ọṣun became a river, and Ọba became another river. At the place where they meet, the water is always agitated. If one crosses one of the rivers, one must not mention the name of the other on pain of drowning. And whence the saying, *Ọba ma bọṣun*, "You cannot sacrifice to Ọba and Ọṣun at the same time." (I would translate this as "Ọba does not sacrifice to Oshun.")

There is also a Yoruba proverb that says, "We don't give the child of Ọba to Oshun" (*A ki gbe ọmọ Ọba fun Ọṣun*).

A second Yoruba version recorded by Verger[10] at Ouidah in Dahomey says that Ṣango had three wives, Ọya, Ọṣun, and Ọba. Ọṣun and Ọba were always fighting. One day Ọba was with Ṣango while Ọṣun was doing the cooking. Ọba told Ọṣun that it was the wish of Ṣango that his food be cooked on a fire made with banana trunks; the fire could not be lit, and when Ṣango returned his meal was not ready. Ṣango was angry. Later it was the turn of Ọṣun to be with Ṣango. In revenge she told Ọba that it was the wish of Ṣango that Ọba's ear be used in preparing his food. When Ṣango returned, he again became angry and fought the jealous wives.

A Yoruba version of the myth reported by Harold Courlander does not mention Ọba.[11] Shango had many wives, including Oya and Oshun. Oya was a good cook, but Oshun's cooking did not please Shango at all, and Oya envied Oshun's beauty. The day of the annual festival was approaching, and as usual Shango would provide a feast. He appointed Oya and Oshun to prepare the food. Oshun asked Oya to tell her how she made her food so tasty. Oya said, "Have you never noticed that I always wear my headdress low to cover my ears?" She said that she had cut off her ears to use as a special ingredient in the food. Oshun cut off her ears and put them in soup. When it was served, one of the guests found her two ears in his bowl and fled in horror. Everyone saw the ears and departed. In disgust and anger, Shango summoned Oya and Oshun. Oya told what Oshun had done, and Shango removed Oshun's headdress. Oshun accused Oya of having cut off her ears also, but when Oya's headdress was removed her ears were unmutilated.

Finally, toward the end of our 1950–51 fieldwork, a diviner recited two versions of the myth into a tape recorder. He belonged to the cult of Orishala at Ọyọ, but he had been trained in divining with sixteen cowries in the town of Igana, where he was born. He agreed to tape all the verses for sixteen cowry divination that he knew, and when he finished he recorded a number of myths. They were recorded in Yoruba, transcribed, and translated.

Both versions of the myth are obviously based on a divination verse, with the names of the mythical diviners (given in quotation marks) interrupting the narrative, but it was not included by him as a verse for sixteen cowry divination. They are told in poetic rather than prose form, and they include an episode not previously encountered. Ifa and Ọrunmila are names of the Yoruba God of Divination.

"The child learns to buy a knife;
"The child buys a very sharp one"
They were the ones who divined for Shango.
He took Ọba as a wife
And chose Ọya as a concubine.
"The vine clings to the tree at the bottom
"And climbs up to the top"
They were the ones who divined for Ọba
Who was the favorite wife of Shango.
She said, "This husband, how will he love me,
"That he will never leave me,
"That he will love me
"And will not love anyone else?
"What should I do?"
And she went (to the diviners),
And they said, "What is it?"
"What should I use in cooking stew?
"What should I use in cooking stew for a husband
"So that he will love me?"
"An ear is what one should cook stew with for a husband,
"So that he will love one."
"Ha! An ear?"
They said, "Yes."
"Can you help me cut it?"
They said, "Yes."
She said they should cut it,
And they cut it;
They cut it.
After they cut off her ear
She cooked it for Shango,
And he ate it.
Inevitably after a while
Ọrunmila took Ọba from Shango.
When he had taken her, what then?
"Wherever you are going
"I will go with you"
Was the one who divined for Ọya

Who succeeded Ọba.
She said she would follow Ọrunmila,
And Ọrunmila married her.
"Little things are what we are seeing;
"A big thing is coming, father of them all"
Was the one who divined for Ọrunmila.
Ifa again said he would marry Oshun.
After he married Oshun, what then?
He married Oshun.
Well, Ọba was his senior wife,
But Ọba was the one who washed the dishes;
Ọba was the one who ground the pepper;
Ọba was the one who cooked the food.
The senior wife!
Ọya just sat down.
After a while Ọya said, "I will open something for you to see,"
And Ọba trembled in fright.
Then Oshun arrived,
And one day
Oshun watched them and watched them.
She called Ọba and asked,
"Why is it that you act like this?"
She said, "This is how Ọya frightens me.
"She says she will open something for me to see."
Oshun said, "You must not grind pepper any more.
"Aren't you the senior wife?
"Well then, can't she grind pepper for me
"As you are grinding pepper for her?"
Oshun came.
When Ọya called, "Ọba, come and do this,"
Oshun would say, "You must not do it."
Ọya would say, "I will open something for you to see."
Oshun said, "What do you have to open?"
Ọya said, "I will open it for you to see."
"Well!" Oshun said, "Open it now.
"Whatever you have to open, open it.
"Today you will open it!
"If you don't open it, you must not leave."
When Ọya opened her skirt
There were sixteen vaginas under her waist,
And all of them were emitting smoke.
When Ọya opened her skirt thus
Oshun said, "Is that all?"
When Oshun opened her skirt,
Sixteen, sixteen times sixteen vaginas

Were under her waist,
And Parrots' tail feathers were her pubic hair,
Bright red.
Ǫba and Ǫya fled in fear.
Ǫba fled;
Ba! Ba! Ǫba was the first to fall down,
And Ǫba became a river.
Gba! Gba! Ǫya fell down,
And she too became a river.
And Ǫshun also fell down,
And she became a river.
That was the day that those three fell down
And that they became rivers.
"The child learns to buy a knife;
"The child buys a very sharp one"
They were the ones who divined for Ǫrunmila.
Ifa took Ǫba as a wife
And chose Ǫya as a concubine.
"The vine clings to the tree at the bottom
"And climbs up to the top"
Was the one who divined for Shango
When he married Ǫya and married Ǫba.
"Little things are what we are seeing;
"A big thing is coming, father of them all"
They were the ones who divined for Ǫrunmila.
Ifa was going to marry Ǫshun.
That is where these three became rivers.

In this first version it seems that Ǫba's diviners were the ones who told her to cut off her ear; in the second it is Ǫya. The first version contains several inconsistencies, but they need not concern us here. The second version follows.

"The child learns to buy a knife;
"The child buys a very sharp one"
Cast for Ǫrunmila.
Ifa took Ǫba as a wife
And chose Ǫya as a concubine.
"The vine clings to the tree at the bottom
"And climbs up to the top"
Cast for Ǫrunmila.
Ifa was courting Ǫshun.
Ǫrunmila took Ǫba as wife
And they were living together.
After a while
Ifa took Ǫya from Shango

And married Oya.
When Orunmila took Oya as a divorcée
Oba was the one who ground pepper for her.
Oba was the one who pounded yam flour;
Oba was the one who pounded yam loaf;
She was the one who prepared food.
Oba was the one who fetched water,
Who swept the house,
And who polished the floor.
Oshun was coming to visit,
And when Oshun came to visit Orunmila,
She was watching them from head to foot (lit., hands and feet).
She said, "You, Oba,
"What is the matter? Who is the senior wife?"
Oba said, "I am,
"But I don't know what is the matter with my husband.
"He loves Oya too much."
When Oba asked Oshun,
Oshun said she should go and ask Oya.
When she asked Oya,
Oya said, "Ha! Your husband cannot love you,
"You who have been with him all these days
"And did not cook your ear for him
"And give it to him to eat.
"If you cut your ear for him
"He will love you."
Oba said they should cut off one of her ears,
And Oba gave it to her husband.
(She told Oshun), "This is what she said,
"You, Oshun, this is what she said."
Oshun said, "Go and do it,"
And she did so.
Oshun said, "I am coming."
When she came
She married Orunmila.
When Oya told Oba to grind pepper,
Oshun would say, "Don't grind it."
When she told her to go to the river,
Oshun would say, "Don't go."
When she said, "Sweep the floor,"
Oshun would say, "Don't sweep it."
When she said she should polish the floor,
Oshun would say, "Don't polish it."
Oya threatened, "I will open something for you to see."
Oshun said, "What do you have to open for me to see?
"What do you have?"

Ọshun said, "Open what you have.
"What you have to open, open it."
When Ọya did so,
She opened her underskirt slowly like this
And from below fire was smoking.
Sixteen vaginas were under her waist
And they were smoking.
Ha!" Ọshun said, "Is that all?"
She said, "I dare you to wait and see mine!"
When Ọshun opened hers slowly like this,
There were sixteen, sixteen times sixteen vaginas.
Parrots' tail feathers were her pubic hair;
They were bright red.
Ọba fled, Ọya fled,
And Ọshun ran after them.
Ọba was the first to fall down,
And Ọba became a river.
Ọshun also fell down and she became a river.
That was the day that these three became rivers.

Some folklorists still maintain that few, if any, African folktales are known in America. While they may be referring only to the United States, they speak of America. But here is a myth about which there can be no question. As told in Cuba and Brazil, it had an African, and specifically a Yoruba, origin. It is Ọba who cut off her ear in all sixteen versions, with the single exception of Courlander's, whose informant seems obviously to be mistaken. The variants differ, even within Cuba, or Brazil, or West Africa; but it makes little difference whether the ear was cooked in stew, soup, or porridge, or whether Ọba was tricked by Ọya or Ọshun. Both of the two latter variations are probably legitimate and, as a hypothesis, I would suggest that worshippers of Shango credit Ọya with the trick, while Ọshun worshippers claim the credit for their own deity; for others, it depends on which variant they heard.

In its different versions, the myth explains and validates various religious beliefs and ritual practices, including the tabus on mixing the waters of the Ọba and Ọshun rivers and on mentioning the name of one when crossing the other; why Ọba and Ọya, or Ọba and Ọshun, are enemies; how Ọba, Ọya, and Ọshun turned into rivers and became river goddesses; and why Ọba dances with her hand on her ear or with her ears covered with leaves or a cloth.

I

Ọmọ kọ́bẹ rà;
Ọmọ rà jónijóni
Àwọn ló dá fún Ṣàngó.

Ó gbé Ọbà níyàwó
Ó sì lọ yan Ọya lálè.
Wònrànwọ́nrán dìmọ́gi nílẹ̀
Ó ba dórí
Àwọn ló dá fún Ọbà
Tí ṣe àyò Ṣàngó.
Òn, ọkọ yi bí o ti ṣe fẹ́ràn òn,
Tí kò fi ní kọ̀ òn lẹ̀,
Tí yió fi fẹ́ràn òn
Ti kò fi lè fẹ́ ẹlòmíràn mọ́?
Òn tí lè ṣe?
Ó sì lọ,
Wọn ní kiní?
Kí lọ̀ fi sebẹ̀?
Kí là fí sebẹ̀ fún ọkọ
Tí fi fẹ́ràn ẹni?
Etí ni à fí sebẹ̀ fún ọkọ,
Tí fí fẹ́ràn ẹni.
Ha! Etí?
Ó ní hin.
Ẹ ó a lè bá òn ke?
Wọn ní han nù.
Ó ní wọn ó ke,
Ni wọn bá ke;
Ni wọn bá ke.
Kí wọn ó ké etí nù un
Ọbà bá sè fún Ṣàngó,
Ó bá jẹ ẹ.
Dandan nà nígbàtí yio pẹ́
Ọrúnmìlà ó gba Ọbà lọ́dọ̀ Ṣàngó.
Nígbàtí yi ó gba títítí ńkọ́?
Níbi ò nrè
Ma bá ọ lọ
Nló dá fún Ọya
Ló tẹ̀lé Ọbà.
Ó ní a fi bí òn na tẹ̀lé Ọrúnmìlà,
Ọrúnmìlà fẹ́ ẹ.
Kékèké là ńrí;
Ñlá ńbọ̀, baba gbogbo wọn
Nlo wá dá fún Ọrúnmìlà.
Ifá tún ni òn ó fẹ́ Ọṣun.
Nígbàtí yí ó fẹ́ Ọṣun ńkọ́?
Ó fẹ́ Ọṣun.
Bẹ̀ e ní Ọbà ni ìyálé,
Ọbà ní fọ̀wo;
Ọbà ní lọta;

Ǫbà ní sè ońję.
Ìyálé!
Ǫya a jókó.
Bó bá pé Ǫya a ní òn ó mǫ ṣí ǹkan,
Ǫbà a mǫ gbǫn.
Nǐgbà tó ṣe Ǫṣun dé,
Nǐgbà ó dijǫ́ kan
Ǫṣun wò wǫn títítí.
Ó wá pé Ǫbà
Ḕ ti rí tí ìwǫ fi nṣe bá un?
Ó ní bí tí ṣe nù un.
A ní òn ó ṣí nkan.
Ó ní ǫ ò gbǫdǫ̀ lǫta mǫ́.
Ṣe bí ìwǫ nìyálé?
Nję kí òn nà ó mǫ wá lǫta fún òn
Bí ìwǫ ti ńlǫta un?
Ǫṣun dé.
Bí Ǫya bá pé Ǫbà o wá ṣe báyí,
Òṣun a ní ǫ̀ gbǫdǫ̀ ṣe.
Ǫya a ní òn ó ṣí ǹkan hàn ǫ́.
Òṣun a ní kiní ǫ ní tí ǫ ṣí?
A ní òn ó ṣi hãn.
Hǫ́wù! Òṣun ní ṣi níbḕ un.
Ntí o bá ni tǫ́ ṣi, ṣí i.
Lóni lǫ̀ ṣi!
Bí ò ṣi o gbǫdǫ̀ lǫ níbḕ un.
Nǐgbà Ǫya o ṣi
Òbò mḛ́rìndílógún ní ńbḛ nídí rḛ̀,
Gbogbo ḛ̀ ní nrúná.
Ti Ǫya ǫ ṣiṣǫ
Ǫṣun ní ó di ení.
Nǐgbàtí Ǫṣun ó ṣi pḛ̀ ḛ̀ báyí,
Mḛ́rìndílógún, mḛ́rìndílógún ǫ̀nà mḛ́rìndílógún
Ní ńbḛ nídí rḛ̀,
Ḕkó ódḛ ni irun rḛ̀,
Ó wá bḛ yò ò.
Ǫbà òn Ǫya bá họ.
Ǫbà họ;
Bà! Bà! Ǫbà ló kǫ́ lù ilḛ̀,
Ǫbà di odò.
Gbà! Gbà! Ǫya nà lùlḛ̀,
Òn nà di odò.
Ni Ǫṣun nà bá lùlḛ̀,
Ló bá di odò.
Nijǫ́ nà ni àwǫn mḛ́tḛ̀ta bá lúlḛ̀

Tí wọn di odò.
Ọmọ kọ́bẹ rà;
Ọmọ rà jónijóni
Àwọn ló dá fún Ọrúnmìlà.
Ifá gbé Ọbà níyàwó
Ó lọ yan Ọya lálè.
Wọ̀nrànwọ́nrán dìmọ́gi nílẹ̀
Ó ba dé orì
Ló dá fún Ṣàngó
Tó fẹ́ Ọya tó sì fẹ́ Ọbà.
Kékèké là ńrí;
Nlánlá ńbọ̀, baba gbogbo wọn
Àwọn ló dá fún Ọrúnmìlà.
Ifá ó fẹ́ Ọṣun.
Ibi tí àwọn mẹ́tẹ̀ta gbé di odò nù un.

II

Ọmọ kọ́ ọ̀bẹ rà;
Ọmọ rà jónijóni
Dá fún Ọrúnmìlà.
Ifá gbé Ọbà ní ìyàwó
Ó yan Ọya lálè.
Wọ̀nrànwọ́nrán dìmọ́ igi nílẹ̀
Ó ba dé orí
Dá fún Ọrúnmìlà.
Ifá nṣe ọ̀rẹ Ọṣun.
Ọrúnmìlà ó gbé Ọbà níyàwó nù un
Wọn ńbá aiyé wọn lọ.
Nĩgbàtí o ṣe
Ifá gba Ọya lọ́dọ̀ Ṣàngó
Kó fẹ́ Ọya.
Nĩgbàtí Òrúnmìlà ó mú Ọya lópó
Ọbà ní nlọ ata fún Ọya.
Ọbà ní gúnlùbọ́;
Òn ní gúnyán;
Òn ní rokà.
Ọbà ní pọnmi,
Ní gbálẹ̀,
Ní palé.
Ọṣun nwã nwa wá,
K'Ọṣun o ma wá Ọrúnmìlà wa nun,
Nwò wọn l'ọ́wọ́, nwò wọn lẹ́sẹ̀.
Ó ní iwọ Ọbà
Ẹ ti jẹ́? Tani ìyálé?
Ọbà ní òn ni,

Òn o sì wá mọ ntóse ti ọkọ òn.
Tí o ṣe fẹ́ràn Ọya tó bá un.
Nígbàtí Ọbà ó bi Ọṣun,
Ọṣun ní kó lọ bi Ọya.
Nígbàtí yió bi Ọya
Ọya ni Ha! Ọkọ ò lè fẹ́ràn ìwọ,
Ìwọ tí o ti dé ọ̀dọ̀ rẹ̀ látijọ́ yi
Tí ọ fi etí sebẹ̀ fun
Kí o fun jẹ.
Tí o bá fi etí sebẹ̀ fun
Yió fẹ́ràn rẹ.
Ọbà ní kí wọn ó fá òn letí kan,
Ọbà sì fi fún ọkọ.
Bó ti wí nìyi,
Ìwọ Ọṣun bó ti wí nìyi.
Ọṣun ní lọ rè ṣe bẹ́ ẹ̀,
Ó sá ṣe bẹ̀ ẹ̀ nù un.
Ọṣun ní òn bọ̀ wá.
Nígbàtí yió wa
Ó wá fẹ́ Ọrúnmìlà.
Bí Ọya bá ní kí Ọbà ó lọta,
Ọṣun a ní kí ó mọ́ lọ.
Tí ó bá pé kó lọ odò,
A ní kí ó mọ́ lọ.
Bó ní gbálẹ,
A ní kí ó mọ́ gba.
Bí ó pé ki ó pa ilé,
A ní kí ó mọ́ pa.
Òn ó mọ̀ ṣí nkan hàn ọ.
Kí lọ ó a ṣí hàn òn?
Kí lọ ní?
Ọṣun ní ṣí on tí o ní.
Òn ti ọ o ṣí ó ní ṣi.
Nígbàtí Ọya ó ṣe,
Ọya ṣí tòbí ẹ̀ pẹ́ ẹ báyí
Gbogbo abẹ́ ẹ̀ ni iná ńrú.
Òbò mẹ́rìndílógún ní ńbẹ ní ìdí Ọya
Iná ní ńrú níbẹ̀.
Ha! Ọṣun nnà ní kíni?
Ó ní ọ ò yó a dúró ọ wò tòhun!
Nígbàtí Ọṣun ó ṣí ti ẹ̀ pẹ́ báyí,
Mẹ́rìndílógún, mẹ́rìndílógún ọ̀nà mẹ́rìndílógún.
Ẹkó ídẹ ló i ṣe irun rẹ̀;
Ni iho ẹ bẹ sò.
Ọbà ọ Ọya ọ,

Ọ̀ṣun nà gbá yá wọn.
Ọ̀bà ló kọ́ lùlẹ̀,
Ló bá di odò.
Ọ̀ṣun nà bá lùlẹ̀ ló bá di odò.
Ijọ́ tí àwọn mẹ́tẹ̀ta ti wọn dodò nù un.

NOTES

1. Lydia Cabrera, *El Monte. Igbo Finda, Ewe Orisha, Vititi Nfinda,* 2d ed. (Miami: Colección del Chicherekú, 1968), pp. 224–26.

2. Romulo Lachatañeré, "El Sistema Religioso de los Lacumís y otra Influencias Africanas en Cuba. III," *Estudios Afrocubanos,* 5 (1945–46), 208. A similar version, discovered too late to be included in this analysis, has been published by Mercedes Cros Sandoval in *La Religion Afrocubana* (Madrid: Playor, 1975), pp. 211–12.

3. Roger Bastide, *Le Candomblé de Bahia (Rite Nagô),* Le Monde d'Outre Mer, Passé et Présent, Première Série, Études V (1968), p. 176.

4. Edison Carneiro, "Xango," in *Novos Estudos Afri-Brasileiros,* ed. G. Freyre et al., Biblioteca de Divulgação Scientifica, IX, Civilização Brasileira (1937), pp. 143–44.

5. Edison Carneiro, *Candomblés de Bahia,* Publicações do Museu do Estado, No. 8 (1948), p. 46.

6. Pierre Verger, *Dieux d'Afrique, Culte des Orishas et Vodouns à l'ancienne Côte des Esclaves en Afrique et à Bahia, la Baie de tous les Saints au Brésil* (Paris: Paul Hartmann Éditeur, 1954), pp. 185–86.

7. Bastide, pp. 176–77.

8. William Bascom, *Shango in the New World,* Occasional Publication of the African and Afro-American Research Institute, No. 4 (Austin: The University of Texas at Austin, 1972), p. 14.

9. Pierre Verger, *Notes sur le Culte des Oriṣa et Vodun à Bahia, la Baie de tous les Saints, au Brésil et à l'ancienne Côte des Esclaves en Afrique,* Mémoires de l'Institut Français d'Afrique Noire, No. 51 (1957), p. 413.

10. Ibid.

11. Harold Courlander, *Tales of Yoruba Gods and Heroes* (New York: Crown Publishers, 1973), pp. 87–90.

PUTTIN' DOWN OLE MASSA:
AFRICAN SATIRE IN THE NEW WORLD

William D. Piersen

Considering the substantial scholarship examining both the resistance of American slaves to bondage and their musical contribution to American culture, it is surprising that more attention has not been paid to the satirical songs and mimicry used by black bondsmen to lampoon the shortcomings of their white masters.[1] Only a small segment of Afro-American satiric commentary was directed against the white ruling class; nonetheless, this aggressive use of ridicule against the white power structure is one of the most interesting examples of the African cultural institutions that survived in the New World. The explicit exercise of satiric derision was a safety valve for the frustrations boiling out of the repressed and exploited Afro-American subculture. But more than this, black slaves were able to manipulate the behavior of their white masters by judiciously tempering their satire with songs of flattery.

Africanists have long recognized the cultural significance of satire in African societies, and the influence of the derisive song as a mechanism of social control.[2] Improvisational musical composition seems to have been ubiquitous in Africa. Traditional associations, master-singers, work groups, and individual villagers all composed songs satirically alluding to complaints against neighbors and relatives, great men and rulers; moreover, Africans seemed especially to enjoy lampooning the Europeans with whom they had dealings. Through the satire of derisive songs, African societies discouraged unpleasant and dangerous face-to-face confrontations. Instead, social etiquette allowed a safer, more effective, and certainly more entertaining manner of criticism. The satiric song carried the propriety of custom and good manners. Private slights were not allowed to fester, neither were the great and powerful permitted to remain immune from the complaints of the weak, as grievances and frustrations were aired before the bar of public opinion. The victim of ridicule was obliged to grin and bear the allusions in somewhat the same manner that in Western culture a man must be able to take a joke at his expense while, on the other hand, he is expected to revenge an insult. If some African societies limited much of their political satire to holiday festivals or special situations, the satiric songs of more personal gossip and recrimination were a part of everyday life. Such satire was especially refined by the bardic "griots" of African society who were renowned for their praise-songs but also feared for the sharp deflating barbs of their wit.

Throughout much of Africa, songs used for social control still lampoon the pompous and condemn those who neglect their duties, or who are cruel and overbearing. "One can well imagine," says Hugh Tracey in his study of Chopi musicians, "the forcefulness of the reprimand conveyed to a wrong doer when he finds his misdeeds sung . . . before all the people of a village, or the blow to the pride of an overweening petty official who has to grin and bear it while the young men jeer to music at his pretentiousness."[3] What better sanction, he wonders, against those who outrage the ethics of a community than to know they will be pilloried by the barbs of a master-singer and the general laughter of the public. In such songs, cleverly veiled but pointed references to the sources of social injustice are broadcast throughout the marketplace to the widespread enjoyment and satisfaction of the public.[4]

Among the Ashanti such satire was directly institutionalized in the *apo* and similar ceremonies, where ridicule of authority was especially sanctioned and encouraged for a limited period.[5] William Bosman observed just such an annual festival at Axim on the Gold Coast at the beginning of the eighteenth century, where, he reports, for eight days a perfect liberty of lampooning was allowed; indeed, "scandal is so highly exalted, that they may freely sing of all the faults, villainies, and frauds of their superiors as well as inferiors, without punishment, or so much as the least interruption; and the only way to stop their mouths is to ply them lustily with drink, which alters their tone immediately, and turns their satirical ballads into commendatory songs on the good qualities of him who hath so nobly treated them."[6]

But African satire was not only political. John Atkins noted in 1721 that as part of the diversion of evening entertainments the inhabitants of Sierra Leone would gather in an open part of town to form "all round in a circle laughing, and with uncouth notes, blame or praise somebody in the company."[7] Africans used satiric song to burlesque domestic quarrels and neighborly disputes as well as to hew villagers to the line of proper social conduct. As Brodie Cruickshank observed from the Gold Coast in the nineteenth century, such songs were often improvised by singers who were "very expert in adapting the subjects of [their] songs to current events, and [who] indulge in mocking ridicule, in biting sarcasm, in fulsome flattery, or in just praise of men and things, according as circumstances seem to demand." As Cruickshank explained: "This habit of publishing the praise, or shame of individuals in spontaneous song, exercises no little influence upon conduct."[8] Africans, like all men, were susceptible to flattery and in dread of ridicule.

And as the press is feared and courted in America, so too were the improvisational singers of Africa who served as the organs of public opinion in traditional nonliterate society.

Worksongs were a favorite vehicle for African satire. For this reason visitors to Sierra Leone in the eighteenth and nineteenth centuries found the songs of native boatmen particularly entertaining. To the stroke of the oars a lead singer among the rowers would boom out an impromptu couplet, and his crew would respond in a general chorus. The songs boasted the exploits of the rowers, and lampooned females of their acquaintance; they also broadcast the news of the coast and added gossipy satires of current events. Sometimes the sarcasm of the crew was more pointedly directed at their employers or the important men of their society. As Thomas Winterbottom observed in the 1790s, the songs were often "of a satirical cast lashing the vices of the neighboring *head men*."[9] While it may have been safer to criticize neighboring leaders, the allusions were of unmistakably wider application. Subtlety and wry indirection are the requirements of African verbal wit, and the demonstration of verbal skill more than circumspection demanded a satire by allusion. The rowers were not afraid to be more direct in their comments; as Winterbottom notes, the impromptu songs of the boatmen "frequently describe the passengers in a strain of praise or of the most pointed ridicule."[10]

Satire has continued to function in African society as an important way of releasing frustrations that would otherwise be repressed. The satiric functions of the "amusing spirits" of the *Poro* society of Sierra Leone or the topical songs and pantomime of the *Ogo* society of eastern Nigeria both remain part of a continuous line of African satiric commentary with marked similarity to Afro-American examples.[11] Also akin to Afro-American holiday songs, the satiric commentary of the "spirits" of Sierra Leone and the more formal satiric invective of Hausa praise-singers of northern Nigeria display a quality of blackmail, since the important persons honored by the attentions of the singers must come up with a gift or money to avoid being publicly mimed or criticized. Great generosity to the spirits of praise-singers is the expected behavior and, therefore, is not regarded as a response to potential extortion, but, rather, as a worthwhile display of social prestige naturally rewarded with fitting songs of praise.[12]

Five worksong texts recorded by Alan Merriam from Bashi girls on a coffee and quinine plantation in the Kiv area of the then Belgian Congo in the 1950s are particularly suggestive in their relationship to the praise and satire in New World plantation worksongs discussed later in this article. The girls directed their songs at the owner of the plantation who was serving as interpreter of the texts. He had recently stopped giving his workers rations of salt and peanut or palm oil because of an advance in their wages. The singers, reports Merriam, began by indicating the plantation setting; they followed with songs of flattery until in the fourth song the question of the salt and oil rations was raised. In the final song the girls threatened to take jobs elsewhere if the rations were not reinstated. The songs had informed the owner of a discontent that he had not realized existed among his workers. The girls had been unwilling to complain directly, but through the medium and progression of the songs they had been able to express their unhappiness.[13]

Whites have always been a favorite target of African satire, and Europeans in Africa commonly were lampooned as objects of native humor and mimicry. Early Portuguese and French missionaries on the slave coast, for example, were badly discouraged to find themselves and their services mocked in native frolics led by their best catechism pupils.[14] European traders fared little better, as they were universally victims of improvised satiric songs. Brodie Cruickshank noted that on the Gold Coast a passing white man was soon caricatured by the improvisational talents of native songsters: "They would quickly seize some peculiarity of his character whether good or bad, and celebrate it aloud, amidst the unrestrained merriment of the bystanders."[15] A. B. Ellis explained the same situation later in the nineteenth century, noting that "it is not uncommon for singers to note the peculiarities of persons who may pass, and improvise at their expense. This is particularly the case when the strangers are European, as the latter do not . . . understand Tshi, and the singers can allow themselves greater latitude than would be the case if their remarks were understood."[16] Mungo Park recorded the words of such a song during his Niger expedition of 1796. A young woman spinning cotton commented on Park's arrival to the women of her work group who joined her in the chorus: "The winds roared, and the rains fell. The poor white man, faint and weary, came and sat under our tree. He has no mother to bring him milk; no wife to grind his corn. Let us pity the white man; no mother has he."[17] Captain Hugh Clapperton was witness to a more cutting lampoon of the whites while visiting the Yoruba in 1826 during a special series of plays given in honor of his arrival. The third act featured a "white devil" which, Clapperton reports,

> went through the motions of taking snuff, and rubbing its hands; when it walked, it was with the most awkward gait, treading as the most tender-footed white man would do in walking barefoot, for the first time over new frozen ground. The spectators often

> appealed to us, as to the excellence of the performance . . . I pre-
> tended to be fully as pleased with this caricature of a white man
> as they could be, and certainly the actor burlesqued the part to
> admiration.[18]

In the 1860s, Richard Burton likewise found his note-taking to be an object of mime and satire by the jesters of Dahomey.[19] In the recent past, companies recording West African tunes sung by Africans in European ports discovered that this tradition has continued, for the songs sold well in West Africa precisely for their biting satire of white society.[20]

Thus it should not be surprising that throughout the New World during the slaving era Afro-American bondsmen would display a genius for improvising songs lampooning the foibles of their masters and advertising harsh or unfair treatment before the general censure of society. Bryan Edwards observed that blacks in the eighteenth-century West Indies adopted a special genre of improvised ballad for their "merry meetings and midnight festivals," where they gave "full scope to a talent for ridicule and derision, . . . exercised not only against each other, but also, not infrequently, at the expense of their owner or employers."[21] James Phillippo noted at the beginning of the nineteenth century that in Jamaica such songs "had usually a ludicrous reference to the white people, and were generally suggested by some recent occurrence."[22] As Richard R. Madden explained, the Afro-American facility for extemporaneous song-making and sarcastic mimicry was extraordinary: "They are naturally shrewd and quick observers, fond of imitation, and wonderfully successful in practicing it. I think they have the best perception of the ridiculous of any people I ever met."[23]

The African provenience of the satiric slave songs is suggested not only by their wry content, improvisational style, leader and response pattern, and general performance, but also by their wide diffusion throughout the New World, spanning areas dominated by a variety of European cultures in the colonial era.

On the British island of St. Christopher, Clement Caines recorded that "the Negroes dress every occurrence in rhyme, and give it a metre, rude indeed, but well adapted to the purposes of raillery or sarcasm."[24] Sometimes the satire was cruel; one of the most interesting examples was recorded in British Jamaica at the beginning of the nineteenth century. Robert Renny reports that Europeans arriving at the dock in Port Royal were met by a boat of black women selling fresh fruits and singing the strangest advertising jingle on record.

> New-come buckra,   [white man]
>   He get sick,
> He take fever.
>   He be die.
>   He be die.
> New-come buckra
>   He get sick, . . .[25]

Perhaps the harshness of this song is partially explained in another in which Jamaican slaves commemorated the infamous conduct of a local master who threw his critically ill slaves into a gully to die after stripping them of their belongings. One of the slaves recovered fleeing to Kingston where he was later discovered by his master who immediately reclaimed him. But when the full story came out, it was the master who was driven from Kingston. And so, when Monk Lewis recorded this song over a quarter of a century later in 1817, the slaves sang:

> Take him to the Gulley! Take him to the Gulley!
>   But bringee back the frock and board.—
> Oh! massa, massa! me no deadee yet!—
> Take him to the Gulley! Take him to the Gulley!
>   Carry him along.[26]

Things seem to have been much the same on the French islands, for in the seventeenth century Jean Baptiste Dutertre described the Africans of the French West Indies as "satirists who reveal even the slightest faults of our Frenchmen [who] cannot do the least reprehensible thing without [the blacks] making it the subject of amusement among themselves. In their worksongs, they repeat all their masters or overseers have done to them, good or bad."[27] Father Jean Baptiste Labat had noticed the same characteristics on his travels. The blacks, he said, "are satirical to excess, and few people apply themselves with greater success to knowing the defects of people, and above all of the whites, to mock among themselves."[28]

Afro-American ridicule and censure gained force through musical presentation. Much like proverbs set to music, improvisational lampoons of the moment were often transformed into pieces of traditional folk wisdom, enjoyed and remembered in good part for the melodies connected to them. As Lafacadio Hearn noted in late nineteenth-century Martinique, "vile as may be the motive, the satire, the malice, these chants are preserved for generations by the singular beauty of the air, and the victim of a carnival song need never hope that his failings or his wrong will be forgotten; it will be sung long after he is in his grave."[29]

In Spanish Cuba, J. G. F. Wurdemann observed that such songs were often combined with dancing, and he reported that "in their native dialects [the slaves] ridicule their owners before their faces enjoying with much glee their happy ignorance of the burthen of their songs."[30]

But generally it does not seem to have mattered if the victim of the songs understood that they were being burlesqued. In fact, Edward Long reported that having a nearby overseer listen to the derision directed at him "only serves to add poignancy to their satire, and heightens, the fun."[31] Thus on the Haitian island of La Gonave, when the leading citizen landowner—a mulatto named Constant Polynice—hosted a Congo Dance, his guests lampooned him with a song.

> Polynice the tax collector.
> Rides at night on his white horse.
> We will drive him away with stones,
> And a misfortune will strike him.

Despite the lyrics, Polynice was generally well liked, and he apparently accepted the song without malice, smiling as if he would have been hurt not to have been so honored.[32]

In Portuguese Brazil, Afro-American slave gangs used their festivals and worksongs to comment on their own foibles, as well as those of their masters, overseers, and slave drivers—often in the riddle form of a *jongo* under the direction of a master-singer of the work gang, who would disguise his allusions where necessary with African words or by transforming his targets metaphorically into animals or trees.[33]

Sometimes the New World satires had an insurrectionary intent. Mrs. Carmichael heard such a "funny song" in Trinidad in the early 1830s, which ridiculed the whites' inability to stop the fires set by maroons in the hillside sugar cane:

> Fire in de mountain
> Nobody for out him   [no one will put it out]
> Take me daddy's bo tick   [dandy stick]
> And make a monkey out him   [let a monkey put it out]
> Poor John! nobody for out him . . .   [poor John Bull][34]

Among themselves, North American slaves also enjoyed parodying their owners in mime and music. A South Carolinian was scandalized when he secretly beheld a Saturday night country dance of the blacks near Charleston in 1772. "The entertainment," he reports, "was opened by the men copying (or taking off) the manners of their masters, and the women those of their mistresses, and relating some highly curious anecdotes, to the inexpressible diversion of that company."[35] Despite his complaints, South Carolina slaves continued to parody their masters into the nineteenth century. A "street girl" from Beaufort explained in the 1840s that "us slaves watch the white folks' parties when the guests danced a minuet and then paraded in a grand march. Then we'd do it too, but we used to mock 'em, every step. Sometimes the white folks noticed it but they seemed to like it. I guess they thought we couldn't dance any better."[36] Whites always seemed slightly flattered and amused by the awkward imitations of black society to duplicate their manners, and always thought it was part of the blacks' character to enjoy even the ungainliest of imitation. Many masters may never have wished to realize there was more than one dimension to slave foolishness.

In the late eighteenth century, lower-class New Englanders thought the election day celebrations of Yankee slaves one of the high points of the social year. After the official colonial or state election ceremonies, slaves were given free time to hold their own election wherein the blacks selected a king or governor of their own community. Whites found the imitation of their own procedures especially amusing and thoroughly enjoyed witnessing the music, dancing, and general tumult of the festivities. The highlight of Black Election was a grand parade and training of troops by the black leaders, which mirrored the white election observances that had taken place such a short time before. Whites always found ludicrous the consummate dignity of the black officials garbed in makeshift and borrowed uniforms, and escorted by a motley troop of fellow slaves firing salutes, pounding drums, and blaring forth every other sort of musical accompaniment. It seemed even more ridiculous, of course, when the black troops would take the command "Fire and fall off" literally—tumbling from their horses onto the common field. Such parodies of the pretensions of both white and black society were considered fun, and since this was a day of license and freedom for the slaves, masters did not interfere until "the utmost verge of decency had been reached, good-naturedly submitting to the hard hits leveled against themselves, and possible profiting a little by some shrewd allusion."[37] Incidentally, the satiric function of these election parades in New England finds an interesting parallel in the *chaluska* Mardi Gras dance in Haiti where the participants dressed as nineteenth-century generals to achieve the effect of comic mimicry.[38]

The foolishness of the slaves in their pastimes reflects the traditional wisdom of the jester that satire is safer and more effective when veiled as coming from the mouth of a fool. Charles William Day noted how, during Carnival in nineteenth-century Trinidad, black celebrants lampooned the slave condition to the general enjoyment of black and white.[39] But James Phillippo observed how Jamaican blacks used this self-parody and feigned ignorance to their own advantage:

> The lowest and most unintelligent of the tribes are Mungolas. Their stupidity, however, has often been more feigned than real; thus, when attracting the gaze of the multitudes at their annual carnivals by their grotesque appearance and ridiculous gambols, they have often been known to indulge in the keenest satire and merriment at their own expense, repeating in chorus, "Buckra tink Mungola nigger fool make him tan so."[40]

A satire of a master did not seem so dangerous when it followed on the heels of a self-parody of the slave condition or a series of praise-songs flattering the master's vanity. Consider the progression of a Louisiana slave song:

> Negro cannot walk without corn in his pocket,
>   It is to steal chickens.
> Mulatto cannot walk without rope in his pocket,
>   It is to steal horses.
> White man cannot walk without money in his pocket,
>   It is to steal girls.[41]

In satire the slaves were able to use their own weakness to best advantage; perhaps that is why the satiric resistance of bondsmen in the American South was not repressed. As Nicholas Cresswell reported in 1774, the blacks of Nanjemoy, Maryland, sang to their banjos a "very droll music indeed. In their songs they generally relate the usage they have received from their masters or mistresses in a very satirical style and manner."[42] William Faux noted this same propensity a half century later in 1819 while listening to the worksongs of a chorus of galley slaves in Charleston: "The verse was their own, and abounding in praise or satire, intended for kind or unkind masters."[43]

This ability to transform songs of praise into songs of recrimination was especially important in using improvisational tunes to countervail a master's domination or to win a reward. Black oarsmen in eighteenth-century Louisiana were no different from the Krumen of eighteenth-century Sierra Leone or the oarsmen of nineteenth-century Charleston in alternating praise with sarcasm to create a self-fulfilling prophecy:

Sing lads; our master bids us sing
For master cry out loud and strong
The water with long oar strike
Sing, lads, and let us haste along. . . .

See! See! the town! Hurrah! Hurrah!
Master returns in pleasant mood.
He's going to treat his boys all 'round.
Hurrah! hurrah for master good.[44]

Even in Louisiana the hint that a good master treats his slaves could hardly be missed. When patriarchal southern masters permitted their servants an entertainment, as at Christmas or corn-shucking time, they would often encourage their bondspeople to sing for them. And, as with similar entertainments in Africa, the singers required a treat for their efforts. Sometimes the slaves went from plantation to plantation, like the John Canoers of North Carolina and Jamaica, singing satiric frolic and praise-songs before demanding small rewards.[45] At other times, the subject of recompense was approached indirectly, but not without more than a trace of humor. As Robert Shepard recalled, the slaves at a corn shucking sang, "Oh! my head, my poor head. Oh! my poor head is affected!" But as Shepard explained, "Dere weren't nothing wrong with our heads. Dat was just our way of lettin' our overseer know us wanted some liquor. Purty soon he would come 'round with a big horn of whiskey, and dat made de poor head well, but it weren't long before it got worse again, and den us got another horn of whiskey."[46] Slaves with good masters encouraged their kindness by emphasizing their masters' best traits through flattering songs of praise; but always there was the implicit threat to turn this praise around. As one black sang:

Massa's nigger am slick and fat,
    Oh! Oh! Oh!
Shine jes like a new beaver hat,
    Oh! Oh! Oh! . . .

Jones' niggers am lean an po'
    Oh! Oh! Oh!
Don't know whether they git 'nough ter eat or no,
    Oh! Oh! Oh![47]

Few masters could resist critical comments on fellow whites (even knowing they should not have been permitted) when they came as part of such gratifying praise. But neither should they have missed the implications about slave owners who neglected the needs of their bondsmen. Slaves might report the derelictions of ol' massa Jones when they had a master nearer to home in mind, just as the bondsmen of Sierra Leone complained about neighboring headmen, and the blacks of Trinidad ridiculed the governments of neighboring islands.[48] The slaves, if not their masters, understood such complaints to be local satires rather than literal criticisms of neighboring leaders.

Of course, not all masters got off easily with songs of praise or veiled allusions. Frederick Douglass records that bitter derision also appeared in frolic songs. It was clear enough when the slaves sang:

> We raise de wheat,
> Dey gib us de corn;
> We bake de bread,
> Dey gib us de crust;
> We sif de meal,
> De gib us de huss;
> We peal de meat,
> Dey gib us de skin;
> And dat's de way,
> Dey take us in;
> Dey skim de pot,
> Dey gib us de liquor,
> And say dat's good enough for nigger.[49]

Even a well-thought-of master had to be careful of his behavior or face ridicule. When Ned Lipscomb, described by one of his slaves as "de best massa in de whole country," ran off to avoid Sherman's army during the Civil War, his slaves memorialized him in a song beginning:

> White folks, have you seed old massa
> Up the road, with he mustache on?
> He pick up he hat and he leave real sudden
> And I believe he's up and gone.
>
> Old massa run away
> And us darkies stay at home.
> It must be now dat Kingsom's comin'
> And de year of Jubilee. . . .[50]

African satire transferred easily to the New World. Unable to develop formal methods of social regulation under the interdictions of bondage, slaves were quick to adopt the informal controls which accompanied public satire, praise, and ridicule. By cleverly intermixing criticism of their masters with flattery and by combining their praise and criticism with equally ridiculous lampoons of black behavior, Afro-

American bondsmen desensitized the seeming impropriety of black slaves satirizing the society of their white owners.[51] Thus, in their songs slaves were able to voice subtly their grievances before their masters and openly vent their frustration and disdain as well. And by commenting on the virtues and foibles of white society, the slaves were sometimes able to improve their own situations, for few masters preferred the barbs of ridicule to the satisfaction of flattery. We have long known that slaves adept at dissembling behavior relished "puttin' on Ole Massa," as it was known, but there was more to African wit than the clever lie, and in the satire of song and pantomime, slaves not only put Ole Massa on, they put him down as well.

NOTES

1. The first scholarly recognition of the satiric song as a category of Afro-American folksong came in the chapter "Satirical Songs of the Creoles," in Henry E. Krehbiel, *Afro-American Folksongs* (New York: G. Schirmir, 1914), pp. 140–53. An important modern study concerned in part with such songs is Harold Courlander, *The Drum and the Hoe* (Berkeley: Univ. of California Press, 1960), chapters 12–13; and a general summary discussion is available in Richard A. Waterman and William R. Bascom, "African and New World Negro Folklore," in *Dictionary of Folklore, Mythology and Legend*, ed. Maria Leach (New York: Funk and Wagnalls, 1949), I, 21. A relevant article is Theodore Van Dam, "The Influence of the West African Song of Derision in the New World," *African Music*, I (1954), pp. 53–56, which connects such early Afro-American songs to the American "blues" and a variety of West Indian music.

2. Alan P. Merriam, "African Music," in *Continuity and Change in African Culture*, ed. William R. Bascom and Melville J. Herskovits (Chicago: Phoenix Books, 1963), pp. 51, 55; Alan P. Merriam, "Music and the Dance," in *The African World*, ed. Robert A. Lystad (New York: Praeger, 1965), pp. 464–66; Waterman and Bascom, "African and New World Negro Folklore," p. 21; and Melville J. Herskovits, *The New World Negro* (Bloomington: Minerva Press, 1969), pp. 137–40.

3. Hugh Tracey, *Chopi Musicians: Their Music, Poetry, and Instruments* (New York: Oxford Univ. Press for the International African Institute, 1948), p. 3.

4. Herskovits, *New World Negro*, p. 138.

5. R. S. Rattray, *Ashanti* (Oxford: Clarendon Press, 1923), I, 151–71.

6. William Bosman, *A Description of the Gold Coast of Guinea* (London: J. Knapton, 1704), p. 158. See also John Barbot, "A Description of the Coasts of North and South Guinea . . . and of the Coast of Angola," in *A*

Collection of Voyages and Travels, ed. Awnsham and John Churchill (London: H. Linton, 1746), V, 317.

7. John Atkins, *A Voyage to Guinea, Brazil, and the West Indies* (1735; rpt. London: Frank Cass, 1970), p. 53.

8. Brodie Cruickshank, *Eighteen Years on the Gold Coast of Guinea* (London: Hurst & Blackelt, 1853), II, 265–66.

9. Thomas Winterbottom, *An Account of the Native African in the Neighborhood of Sierra Leone* (1803; rpt. London: Frank Cass, 1969), I, 112. A similar description can be found in Horatio Bridge, *Journal of an African Cruiser* (New York: Geo. Putnam, 1853), pp. 16–17.

10. Winterbottom, I, 112.

11. Kenneth Little, *The Mende of Sierra Leone* (New York: Routledge & Kegan, 1967), pp. 247–51; and Phoebe Ottenberg, "The Afikpo Ibo of Nigeria," in *Peoples of Africa*, ed. James L. Gibbs, Jr. (New York: Holt, Rinehart and Winston, 1966), pp. 14–15, 34.

12. Little, *The Mende*, p. 251; and M. G. Smith, "The Social Functions and Meaning of Hausa Praise-Singing," in *Peoples and Cultures of Africa*, ed. Elliot P. Skinner (Garden City: Doubleday, 1973), p. 561.

13. Alan P. Merriam, "Song Texts of the Bashi," *Zaire*, 8 (1954), 41.

14. James Pope-Hennessy, *Sins of the Fathers* (New York: Capricorn, 1969), p. 167.

15. Cruickshank, *Eighteen Years on the Gold Coast*, p. 266.

16. Alfred B. Ellis, *The Tshi-Speaking Peoples of the Gold Coast of West Africa* (London: Chapman and Hall, 1887), p. 328.

17. Mungo Park, *Travels in the Interior Districts of Africa in the Years 1795, 1796, and 1797* (New York: N. Farlane, 1801), pp. 197–98.

18. Hugh Clapperton, *Journal of a Second Expedition into the Interior of Africa* (1829; rpt. London: Frank Cass, 1966), p. 55. The Yoruba Egungun society continues to produce plays mimicking Europeans; see Janheinz Jahn, *Muntu: An Outline of the New African Culture* (New York: Grove Press, 1961), p. 79.

19. Richard F. Burton, *A Mission to Gelele, King of Dahome* (1864; rpt. New York: Frederick A. Praeger, 1966), p. 130.

20. Herskovits, *New World Negro*, p. 139.

21. Bryan Edwards, *The History of the British Colonies in the West Indies* (London: John Stockdale, 1801), II, 103.

22. James M. Phillippo, *Jamaica: Its Past and Present State* (Philadelphia: James M. Campbell, 1843), p. 75.

23. Richard R. Madden, *A Twelvemonth's Residence in the West Indies during the Transition from Slavery to Apprenticeship* (Philadelphia: Carey, Lea & Blanchard, 1835), I, 107, and II, passim.

24. Clement Caines, *The History of the General Council and General Assembly of the Leeward Islands* (St. Christopher: R. Cable, 1804), p. 111.

25. Robert Renny, *An History of Jamaica* (London: J. Cawthorn, 1807), p. 241.

26. Matthew G. Lewis, *Journal of a West India Proprietor* (London: J. Murray, 1834), p. 322.

27. Jean Baptiste Dutertre, *Historie générale des Antilles habitées par les François* (Paris: T. Iolly, 1671), II, 497. It was the same for black work-songs in Jamaica in the early twentieth century; see Walter Jekyll, *Jamaican Song and Story* (Nendeln: Folk-Lore Society Pubs., 1967), p. 188.

28. Jean Baptiste Labat, *Noveau voyage aux isles de l'Amerique* (La Haye: P. Husson, 1724), pp. 57–58.

29. Lafacadio Hearn, *Two Years in the French West Indies* (1890; rpt. Boston: Houghton Mifflin, 1922), pp. 250–51.

30. J. G. F. Wurdemann, *Notes on Cuba* (Boston: James Munroe, 1844), p. 84. Satire was also connected to the calenda dance in the French West Indies; see M. L. E. Moreau de Saint-Méry, *Description . . . de la partie française de l'Isle Saint-Dominique* (Philadelphia: by the author, 1797), I, 44.

31. Edward Long, *The History of Jamaica* (London: T. Lowndes, 1774), II, 423.

32. William Seabrook, *The Magic Island* (New York: Harcourt, Brace & Co., 1929), pp. 225–26. For an example of a white judge in New Orleans who was lampooned precisely for the kind of dance he hosted, see George Washington Cable, "The Dance in Place Congo," in *The Negro and His Folklore*, ed. Bruce Jackson (Austin: Univ. of Texas Press for the American Folklore Society, 1967), p. 207.

33. Stanley J. Stein, *Vassouras: A Brazilian Coffee County 1850–1900* (Cambridge: Harvard Univ. Press, 1957), pp. 206–07. Melville Herskovits has also commented on the satire in Brazilian Carnival songs, *New World Negro*, p. 22.

34. Mrs. Carmichael, *Domestic Manners and Social Conditions of the West Indies* (London: Wittaker, Treacher, & Co., 1833), II, 301. Or see Lewis, *Journal of a West India Proprietor*, p. 288, for the insurrectionary song of the "King of the Eboes."

35. *South Carolina Gazette,* 17 September 1772, as quoted in Peter H. Wood, *Black Majority* (New York: Alfred A. Knopf, 1974), p. 342.

36. Quoted in Marshall and Jean Stearns, *Jazz Dance* (New York: Macmillan, 1968), p. 22. Occasionally in slavery personal mimicry could be dangerous. A Negro slave named Monday was purchased by a white who had been offended by Monday's mimicry of him. The new master immediately ordered his slave flogged, but was foiled by Monday's suicide; see the testimony of D. Harrison, *Minutes of the Evidence taken before a Committee of the House of Commons . . . to Consider . . . the Slave Trade* (1791; rpt. Chicago: Afro-Am Press, 1969), IV, 49.

37. James R. Newhall, *History of Lynn, Essex County Massachusetts* (Lynn: by the author, 1883), p. 49. See also William D. Piersen, "Afro-American Culture in Eighteenth Century New England: A Comparative Examination," Diss. Indiana Univ. 1975, pp. 266–88.

38. Courlander, *Drum and the Hoe*, p. 136.

39. Charles Wm. Day, *Five Years Residence in the West Indies* (London: Colburn & Co., 1852), I, 314.

40. Phillippo, *Jamaica*, p. 80.

41. Lyle Saxon, *Gumbo Ya-Ya* (Cambridge: Harvard Univ. Press, 1945), p. 430.

42. Nicholas Cresswell, *The Journal of Nicholas Cresswell* (New York: The Dial Press, 1924), 29 May 1744, pp. 18–19. For insight into how such songs were originally composed, see James Miller McKim, "Negro Songs," *Dwights Journal of Music*, 21 (August, 1862), 149.

43. William Faux, *Memorial Days in America Being a Journal of a Tour* (London: Simpkins & Marshall, 1823), 7 June 1819, p. 195. Such work-songs were similar throughout the New World; see, for example, Pierre De Vassiere, *Saint-Dominque* (Paris, 1909), pp. 255–75.

44. George Washington Cable, "Creole Slave Songs," in *The Negro and His Folklore*, p. 239. For a similar rowing song from St. Thomas alternating praise with sarcasm, see Trelawny Wentworth, *The West India Sketch Book* (London: 1834), II, 240–42, as quoted in Roger D. Abrahams, *Deep the Water, Shallow the Shore* (Austin: American Folklore Society, 1974), p. 19n.

45. See, for example, Kenneth M. Stampp, *The Peculiar Institution* (New York: Alfred A. Knopf, 1963), p. 386; Lewis, *Journal of a West India Proprietor*, p. 56; and, for a parallel Haitian example, Courlander, *Drum and Hoe*, p. 107.

46. Interview with Robert Shepard in *Life under the "Peculiar Institution,"* ed. Norman R. Yetman (New York: Holt, Rinehart & Winston, 1970), p. 267.

47. Booker T. Washington, *The Story of the Negro* (1904; rpt. New York: P. Smith, 1940), I, 160. See also on such songs, Eugene D. Genovese, *Roll, Jordan, Roll* (New York: Pantheon, 1974), p. 318.

48. Winterbottom, *An Account of the Native African,* I, 112; and Melville J. Herskovits, *Trinidad Village* (New York: Octagon Books, 1964), p. 278.

49. Frederick Douglass, *The Life and Times of Frederick Douglass* (Hartford: James Betts, 1882), p. 181. For a similar example from Louisiana, see Saxon, *Gumbo Ya-Ya*, p. 450.

50. Interview with Lorenzo Ezell in Yetman, *Life under the "Peculiar Institution,"* p. 113.

51. Indeed, Afro-American satiric traditions probably influenced the development of Blackface Minstrelsy in the United States as well as the blues in music. See Robert C. Toll, *Blacking Up: The Minstrel Show in Nineteenth Century America* (New York: Oxford Univ. Press, 1974), pp. 50, 74, 259.

AFRICAN AND AFRO-AMERICAN TALES

Alan Dundes

The study of African elements in the New World includes a wide variety of cultural materials. The scholarship treats art (Thompson), music (Waterman), dance (Kurath), folk speech (Turner, Dalby), proverbs (Campbell), and folktales (Crane, Vance, Ellis, Gerber, Crowley, Dundes, Piersen, Bascom, and Dorson). Sometimes the African and Afro-American parallels involve form but not content; sometimes the content is parallel as well. For example, to "sweet talk" someone appears to be a fairly literal translation of an African idiom just as to "bad mouth" someone is. The actual Twi or Vai words have not survived, but the idioms have become established in English.[1] On the other hand, American English "tote," "juke" as in jukebox, "goober" (peanut), and "chigger" seem to be direct borrowings from African languages. (And if one accepts Dalby's evidence, one might also include "dig," "jive," "hip," "jazzy," "un-huh" and "uh-uh" as Africanisms.)[2]

Although some Africanisms remained intact in the New World, the majority of verbal items had to survive the rigors of translation from an African language into English. It is not surprising that folktales could make the jump from one language to another, even an unrelated one, but it is striking that a fixed-phrase genre like proverbs, so dependent as it is upon the nuances of metaphor, could survive translation. In her 1975 M.A. thesis in folklore, Theo Campbell surveyed a representative sampling of the vast African and Afro-American proverb collections. She found thirty-six Afro-American proverbs with close African analogues. Two of the parallels noted by Campbell are:

> When fish come out a sea an' tell you alligator hab feber, belieb him. (Jamaica)
> If the terrapin comes out of the water and tell you the alligator has sore eyes, believe him. (Haiti)
> If the frog tells you the alligator has sore eyes, believe him. (Trinidad)
> If the fish comes out of the water and says the eyes of the crocodile are one in number, who is going to argue with him. (Hausa)[3]

> No cuss alligator long mout 'till you cross riber. (Jamaica)
> You haven't crossed the river yet; don't curse at the crocodile's mother. (Trinidad)

> If you haven't crossed the stream, you do not curse the alligator's
> mother. (Surinam)
> When you have quite crossed the river, you say the crocodile had
> a bump on its snout. (Ashanti)
> Once you have crossed the river, you can be rude to the croco-
> dile. (Twi)[4]

These parallels are remarkably close, especially if one keeps in mind
the fact that variations existed between different African versions of the
same proverb *before* the proverb arrived in the New World. Also the
translation from an African language into English provided opportunity
for errors to occur. This was the case both in Africa when missionaries
and others first transcribed proverb texts and in the New World where
the proverbs were often recorded by individuals lacking formal linguistic training.

Aside from the stormy debate over the origins of the Negro spiritual
—was it more African or more European (cf. Wilgus)—most of the
heated discussion surrounding possible African origins of Afro-
American culture centers around folktales. Folklorist Richard M. Dorson, in his 1967 essay, "Origins of American Negro Tales," prefaced
to his valuable collection, *American Negro Folktales*, states unequivo-
cally and categorically, "The first declaration to make is that this body
of tales does not come from Africa."[5] In a more recent clarification and
amplification of his views, Dorson concludes "that the African component for folk narrative in the mainland United States is too diminished to warrant much affirmation."[6] Although the reference in the first
quotation is presumably to the "body" of tales collected by Dorson himself, it is clear that Dorson tends to equate his corpus with Afro-
American folktales generally and that he doubts that many such tales
stem from Africa. Inexplicably, Dorson failed to cite much of the previous scholarship concerned with the origin of Afro-American folktales
in his 1967 essay though he does do so in his 1975 review.

One possible reason for the initial omission might have been that the
earlier discussions primarily treated tales in Joel Chandler Harris's Uncle
Remus books. Still there is no real excuse for any scholar seriously
interested in the origins of Afro-American tales not to cite them. T. F.
Crane, a professor at Cornell at the end of the nineteenth century, was
one of the most astute and erudite American students of the folktale.
His essay "Plantation Folk-Lore," which appeared in *Popular Science
Monthly* in 1880, was one of the first serious considerations of the issue.
Other essays of the same period were written by Robert Lee J. Vance
and A. B. Ellis. The essay by Ellis, which also appeared in *Popular*

Science Monthly, at that time (1895) an important outlet for folklore scholarship, was entitled "Evolution in Folklore: Some West African Prototypes of the Uncle Remus Stories." However, the most ambitious attempt to unravel the origins question was made by A. Gerber. His essay "Uncle Remus Traced to the Old World" appeared in the *Journal of American Folklore* in 1893. Gerber indicated that his attempts to trace Afro-American tales back to European and African sources was only a preliminary statement and that he fully intended to publish a comprehensive discussion of the matter in a forthcoming memoir of the American Folklore Society. Unfortunately, that memoir never appeared. Nevertheless, writing in a day before the advent of the modern conveniences of Tale Type and Motif Indices, Gerber's comparisons, despite the fact that they were often limited to the citation of a single parallel from Africa or Europe, were impressively accurate and sound. What needs to be done is for some modern student armed with appropriate indices to review the pioneering efforts made by Crane, Vance, Ellis, Gerber, and others. Also the *total corpus* of Afro-American tales should be examined, not just the tales included in Harris's Uncle Remus anthologies and not just the tales collected by Dorson.

It is no longer a matter of guesswork or opinion as to the origin of a given Afro-American folktale. There are a limited number of possibilities. (1) The tale came from Africa. (2) The tale came from Europe. (3) The tale came from American Indian tradition. (4) The tale arose in the New World as a result of the Afro-American experience there. Of course, it should be mentioned that not every scholar cares that much about origins. From that point of view, it doesn't really matter where the tale came from. The important questions are how does it function for the people who tell it now and what does it mean to them and what can it tell us about anxieties, ideologies, and worldview. The point is simply that if one does care about origins, there are methods and techniques available to study the question with some rigor.

If a folktale is widely reported in Africa and in Afro-American tradition and that same tale is *not* found in Europe, one can only conclude that one has an example of an African/Afro-American folktale. I have previously discussed this type of methodology with respect to folktales found among Afro-Americans and American Indians. There I noted, for example, the tale in which a hero seeks to obtain wisdom or a wife and who does so through the capture of various animals, for example, by duping a serpent into foolishly stretching out so that its great length can be measured—thereby enabling the hero to tie the serpent to the measuring stick (Motif H 1154.6, Task: capturing squirrel and rattlesnake). The tale is not reported in Europe so it can hardly be a European Tale Type. It is found among several southeastern American Indian tribes (e.g., Hitchiti, Natchez, Creek, and Seminole), but it is not reported to any extent in the rest of aboriginal America. I did find a half dozen African versions of the tale. Clearly this is an African/Afro-American Tale Type. Gerber in his 1893 essay argued the tale was African (on the basis of a single Wolof parallel), and I was able to confirm his judgment.[7]

Gerber also suggests that the tale which we now label Motif K 263, Agreement not to scratch, is an African tale. In talking, the trickster makes gestures and scratches without detection. The *Motif-Index* indicates only Jamaican and other West Indian sources besides the Uncle Remus text. Again, Gerber on the basis of a single Wolof text proposed an African origin. However, there are numerous African versions of this tale, a fact that supports Gerber's identification of the tale as African.[8]

Gerber did not comment on every tale in the Uncle Remus canon. For example, there is a tale in *Uncle Remus and His Friends*, entitled "Brother Billy Goat Eats His Dinner," in which a goat pretends to eat a rock. In the *Motif-Index*, we find Motif K 1723, Goat pretends to be chewing rock. Frightens wolf. There is but a single reference following [o] the Motif and that is to the Uncle Remus version. However, the tale was also included in Charles C. Jones's *Negro Myths from the Georgia Coast* published in 1888. Can we say anything about its probable origin? It is *not* reported from Europe, and it *is* reported from Africa.[9] Clearly it is more than likely that this is an African/Afro-American Tale Type.

Let me mention briefly another African/Afro-American Tale Type which I do not believe has yet been properly identified as such. There is a tale in which a rooster or other fowl makes an animal dupe believe that he (the rooster) has had his head nor neck cut off. He has, of course, simply hidden his neck under his wing. The hare or other dupe cuts his off and dies. This is Motif J 2413.4.2, Fowl makes another animal believe that he has had his neck cut off. The tale is fairly widespread in Afro-American tradition. It is *not* reported in Europe, and it *is* reported in Africa.[10] Again, it is reasonable to assume that this is an African/Afro-American Tale Type.

Once we have a complete Tale Type index of all African tales and perhaps also a Tale Type Index for Afro-American tales, it will be a relatively simple matter to ascertain just which tales belong to the African/Afro-American tradition. And this brings me to an important point, namely the critical importance of Tale Type Indices as scholarly tools to be used in the task of determining the probable provenience of folktales.

Dorson, among others, has accused Africanists of not knowing about or not utilizing the presently available Tale Type Indices. I would have to agree with this indictment of Africanists, though to be sure one can think of notable exceptions. Let me cite just one example of an Africanist's failure to make use of standard folktale scholarship. In Herskovits's *Dahomean Narrative*, one finds a tale entitled "Mawu's ways are just." Mawu sends a messenger to earth where he meets a companion. In the first house they visit is a sick child. The parents are crying from lack of sleep. Mawu's messenger gives some powder to a man who administers it to the sick child. The child dies. In the next house visited, Mawu's messenger sets the straw of the house on fire. Finally, at a river bank, Mawu's messenger follows an old man gathering leaves and pushes him into the water where he drowns. The companion, aghast, starts to run off, but Mawu's messenger reveals his true identity and explains, "In the house where I killed the child, if that child had not died, its mother and father would have died when it took its first step. It is Mawu who sent me to destroy that child." He continued, "The family where I burned the house has rich relatives among them. But they buried all their money and their children are poor. So I burned the house, so that when they break the walls to make them anew and begin to dig the foundation, they will find the money." He then explained further that he killed the old man so that a young replacement for a king might be named.

Herskovits offers no comparative notes for this tale, and the unwary reader might logically assume that this is a typical African folktale. As a matter of fact, Susan Feldmann selected it as one of the tales to be included in her paperback anthology, *African Myths and Tales*.[11] Is it an African tale? Even the most casual glance at Aarne-Thompson Tale Type 759, God's Justice Vindicated (The Angel and the Hermit) will provide a definitive answer to the question. According to the Tale Type plot summary, an angel takes a hermit with him and does many seemingly unjust things (repays hospitality by stealing a cup or by throwing his host's servant from a bridge, or by killing the host's son). The angel shows the hermit why each of these was just. Distribution includes Danish, Swedish, Irish, French, Spanish, and Italian versions. No other African versions are cited. There can be no question that this is a European Tale Type which has found its way into Dahomey. There is nothing wrong with collecting African versions of European Tale Types nor with including them in published collections of tales elicited from African informants. But it is misleading to simply report such tales without any indication whatsoever of their European provenience.

Having criticized Africanists for failing to make proper use of a tool like the Aarne-Thompson Tale Type Index, which has been available since 1910, let me hasten to point out several serious deficiencies in this very same Tale Type Index. Just because a tale has been included by Aarne or by Thompson in the Type Tale Index does *not* necessarily guarantee that it is a European Tale Type. Just as Africanists have wrongly assumed that every tale they collect from an African informant must be an African Tale Type, so European folklorists have wrongly assumed that every tale collected from a European informant must be a European Tale Type. For example, in the 1961 revision of the Tale Type Index, we find Tale Type 291, Deceptive Tug-of-war. Small animal challenges two large animals to a tug-of-war. Arranges it so that they unwittingly pull against each other (or one end of the rope is tied to a tree). Thompson's list of versions includes one single Spanish-American version, but all the others are from Afro-America plus three versions from Africa. Actually, Gerber had previously identified this tale as African in his 1893 study, and more recently I listed references to several additional dozen African and Afro-American versions of this tale.[12] The point is that this is unquestionably an African Tale Type, *not* a European Tale Type. Yet the tale has a number in the hallowed Aarne-Thompson system.

Stith Thompson in his "Preface to the Second Revision" of the 1961 Tale Type Index states that African tales are not included. He maintains that the Aarne-Thompson Tale Type Index might appropriately be called "The Types of the Folk-Tale of Europe, West Asia, and the Lands Settled by These Peoples." "It would be a mistake," he writes further, "to think that it could be extended to tales of such areas as central Africa, the North American Indians, or Oceania. Each of those would need an index based strictly upon its own traditions." The implication is thus unmistakably that those Types included in the Aarne-Thompson canon are European or Indo-European Tale Types. Yet, as I have indicated, Aarne-Thompson Tale Type 291, Deceptive Tug-of-war, is an African Tale Type. Similiarly, Aarne-Thompson Tale Type 297A, Turtle's war party, is an American Indian Tale Type. There are no European versions—although it is my personal conviction that the tale is genetically related to Tale Type 130, The Animals in Night Quarters (Bremen City Musicians), and Tale Type 210, Cock, Hen, Duck, Pin, and Needle on a Journey, both of which are widely reported in Europe. The issue here is that the occurrence of Turtle's war party in Japanese tradition is evidently sufficient to qualify the tale for inclusion in the Aarne-Thompson system. The danger once again might be that an unwary or uncritical user of the Aarne-Thompson Tale Type Index might wrongly assume that American Indian versions of Big Turtle's war party were "borrowings" from the European tradition.

What this means to students of the folktale is that each individual tale must be evaluated separately and carefully with respect to origins. Even if a particular tale is included in the Aarne-Thompson index, one cannot necessarily assume that the tale in question is definitely European. Dorson, who tends to rely heavily upon the Tale Type and Motif Indices, is unable to shake the influence of a tale's possessing an Aarne-Thompson number. During a trip to Monrovia, Liberia, Dorson was surprised to hear a Vai tale. He describes his shock in vivid detail. "They began telling folktales, and to my amazement came forth the one about how Turtle made Leopard his Riding Horse. I say to my amazement for, although it had some nice local African touches, such as Leopard being ill with malaria, it belonged to the same type well known in the United States, and which I myself collected from American Negroes, as Rabbit Makes Fox His Riding Horse. Since I had strongly espoused the thesis of European rather than African origins of American Negro folktales, this parallelism gave me a jolt—although of course a folklorist is always prepared to find such examples of diffusion. But which way did the riding-horse story diffuse—from Europe to West Africa and then to North America, or from Europe directly to the United States and thence back to West Africa with ex-slaves returning to Liberia? or did it originate in Africa? or India, where the tar-baby story is supposed to have gotten started?"[13]

Dorson identifies the Tale Type as Aarne-Thompson 72, Rabbit Rides Fox A-courting. Bascom challenged this identification, arguing that the Vai tale in question should more appropriately be identified as Aarne-Thompson Tale Type 4, Carrying the Sham-Sick Trickster, a point which Dorson later conceded in a footnote.[14] However, since the two Tale Types appear to be related—that is, since Tale Type 72 seems to include Tale Type 4, as Thompson's cross-references signal—I shall not be concerned with the finer points of distinguishing the two types. For the sake of argument, let us assume that Dorson is correct in his initial identification of the Vai tale as Aarne-Thompson Tale Type 72. Does this identification "prove" that the tale is European? If we look at the versions listed in the Type Index, we find that, except for one Norwegian version and three Latvian versions plus several other anomalous texts, all of the other versions cited are from the New World, and of these the vast majority are in the Afro-American tradition. Seventeen versions are cited from the West Indies. No versions from Africa are cited, but the failure to include African versions available in print in the Tale Type and Motif Indices has been rightly criticized by Piersen. However, Arewa includes two versions of K 1241, Trickster rides dupe horseback (Arewa 1631), and Clarke cites no less than five, including Tiv and Yoruba versions. Dorson in his discussion of the Vai tale and in his scholarly annotated headnote introducing the text of the tale printed in *African Folklore* evidently failed to consult Clarke, which was after all a doctoral dissertation written at Indiana University.[15] Dorson thereby seems to have failed to follow his own good advice regarding the absolute necessity of consulting the relevant Tale Type or Motif Index in weighing questions of origins. From the evidence available, I should think the logical presumption would be that the tale is an African Tale Type that moved to the New World. It is not widespread in Europe, and it does not occur in India. (It is not at all clear why Dorson should even raise the possibility of this particular Tale Type's originating in India.) In sum, using Dorson's own criteria (for comparative analysis and proper identification) of Tale Type 72, we have convincing evidence of an African origin, not a European origin for this Tale Type.

I do not believe the case of Tale Type 72 to be unique. On the contrary, I strongly suspect that a number of Aarne-Thompson Tale Types will one day be shown to be African, not European. Included among such types may be Tale Type 5, Biting the Foot; 37, Fox as Nursemaid for Bear; 66B, Sham-dead (Hidden) Animal Betrays Self (this is probably an Indo-African Tale Type); 73, Blinding the Guard; 122D, "Let me Catch you Better Game"; 126, The Sheep Chases the Wolf; and 1530, Holding up the Rock.[16] I consider this to be a fairly conservative list, and accordingly I have not mentioned such problematic tales as 55, The Animals Build a Road (Dig Well), and 155, The Ungrateful Serpent Returned to Captivity (this is probably an Indo-African-European Tale Type).

The implications of the present argument are potentially devastating for Dorson's repeated contention that the African component for folk narrative in the mainland United States is too miniscule to warrant notice. Whether one is speaking for Afro-American folktales as a whole or just U.S. Afro-American tales or even restricting oneself to the corpus in Dorson's *American Negro Folktales*, the fact is that it is possible to identify positively a considerable number of African, not European, Tale Types. I do not dispute that Dorson himself managed to find a correspondence of only 10 percent in his attempt to locate African/ Afro-American folktale parallels. What I am suggesting is that Dorson made no full search of the African folktale literature in order to seek such parallels. Theoretically, he was not obliged to make such a full search except for the fact that he adamantly claims a 90 percent European origin of his corpus. Practically the only tale for which he openly acknowledges an African origin is the talking skull story.[17]

By relying too heavily and uncritically upon the Tale Type Index and the *Motif-Index* (which do not sufficiently take into account the huge number of African collections), Dorson fails to recognize African Tale Types. Somehow he assumes that if a tale occurs so much as once in Europe it qualifies as a European Tale Type, regardless of the tale's distribution in Africa. My point is that there are possible, if not probable, African Tale Types which have entered the sacrosanct Aarne-Thompson canon. Moreover, even if a tale is reported in both Europe and Africa, it seems obvious enough that the more likely source of such widespread Afro-American versions of Aarne-Thompson 175, Tarbaby and the Rabbit, or 1074, Race Won by Deception: Relative Helpers, was Africa, not Europe.

Just so there can be no mistake about the present argument, let us briefly consider several tales in Dorson's *American Negro Folktales*. The first tale in the anthology is correctly identified by Dorson as Aarne-Thompson Tale Type 15, The Theft of Butter (Honey) by Playing Godfather. Although the tale is found in Europe, it is not listed at all in Baughman's *Type and Motif Index of the Folktales of England and North America*, which suggests that it is not particularly popular in Anglo-American tradition. However, it is extremely widespread in New World Afro-American tradition, as Dorson notes. Flowers, in "A Classification of the Folktale of the West Indies by Types and Motifs," cites no less than twenty versions from the West Indies. But the tale is also popular in Africa. Besides the five versions in Klipple's 1938 dissertation "African Folk Tales with Foreign Analogues," there are five in Arewa's "A Classification of the Folktales of the Northern East African Cattle Area by Type," four in Lambrecht's "A Tale Type Index for Central Africa," and two more in Clarke's "A Motif-Index of the Folktales of Culture-Area V, West Africa" (under Motif K 401.1, Dupe's food eaten and then blame fastened on him). Certainly the absence of the tale in Anglo-American tradition and the presence of the tale in both African and Afro-American traditions would tend to point to an African origin of the tale. Still, since the tale is reported in both Europe and Africa, can one reasonably determine whether this particular Afro-American tradition has a European or African origin? The answer may lie in looking at the specific details of the versions in question. In Dorson's text—he presents four versions—the first four tales in his anthology—the familiar butter-smearing incident is followed by a fire-jumping ordeal. In theory, the guilty party is supposed to be burned by the fire while the innocent one is not. To my knowledge, this motif does not occur in European versions of Aarne-Thompson 15. At any rate, it is not included in the standard Tale Type synopsis. But in African tradition, we can easily find just such a combination of incidents. For example, in a Kamba tale, hare dupes hyena by greasing him over the whole body and around the mouth with fat. Next morning, to determine who is guilty, a basket is set afire and both hare and hyena are asked to jump over it and "he who falls into the fire is the one who has eaten the goat."[18] Whatever the ultimate origin of Aarne-Thompson Tale Type 15 may be, it is pretty clear that the immediate source of the Afro-American versions that include the fire-jumping (or in some versions a river-jumping) motif is Africa, not Europe. It might be noted that T. F. Crane in 1881, arguing without the benefit of modern folklore apparatus, came to much the same conclusion about the tale.[19]

So the first four tales in Dorson's *American Negro Folktales* may come from Africa. What about the fifth tale, "The Bear Meets Trouble"? In this tale, rabbit dupes bear into falling asleep in a field which rabbit then sets afire. Dorson cites no European parallels but lists several Afro-American parallels and refers to a possible Ibo version listed under Motif K 1055, Dupe persuaded to get into grass in order to learn new dance. Grass set on fire.[20] Piersen, in discussing this tale, confirms its widespread occurrence in Afro-American tradition, but as Dorson justly observes, "Piersen admits there is no conclusive evidence for an African origin of 'Bear Meets Trouble.'"[21] But there is evidence for an African origin of this tale. In 1920, Smith and Dale, in *The Ila-Speaking Peoples of Northern Rhodesia*, reported a tale entitled "Hare deceives Lion and burns him to Death"; moreover, they even go so far as to comment on its similarity to "More Trouble for Brother Wolf" found in *Nights with Uncle Remus* as well as providing several additional African parallels.[22] Again, we have an Afro-American tale with no European analogues but with clear-cut African parallels.

What about the sixth tale in Dorson's collection, "The Bear in the Mudhole"? Dorson indicates that the key Motif is K 562.1, Captive trickster persuades captor to pray before eating. The only two references listed in the *Motif-Index* are from Africa. The seventh tale in Dorson's collection is "Rabbit and Bear Inside the Elephant," for which Crane,

Ellis, and Gerber all cited close African parallels at the end of the nineteenth century.[23] Are there other probable African Tale Types in Dorson's collection? Certainly. Tale 15, "The Deer Escapes from the Fox,"
is either Motif K 622, "Captive plays further and further from watchman and escapes," as Dorson suggests, or Motif K 606, Escape by
singing song. In either case, the *only* references in the Motif-Index are
African and Afro-American. Tale 125, Rangtang, is Motif B 524.1.2,
Dogs rescue fleeing master from tree refuge, which has widespread
popularity in both Africa and Afro-America. Dorson seems to incline
towards Parson's view that it is "a European tale brought over by im-
migrants from the west coast of Africa."[24] But the specific motif of *two*
dogs *with peculiar names* is *not* common in Europe at all. It is extremely common, however, in Africa, as Bascom demonstrates in his discussion of twenty-two versions of the tale.[25]

It is not my intention to examine every single tale in Dorson's ad-
mirable collection nor to dispute the many clear-cut European Tale
Types that have been incorporated into Afro-American tradition. What
I am suggesting is that there are a number of demonstrable African
Tale Types in Dorson's collection and furthermore that many of the
apparent "European" Aarne-Thompson Tale Types may in fact be African Tale Types in disguise. If I am proven correct in my assertion
that Aarne-Thompson Tale Types 5, 72, 73, 291, etc., are truly African Tale Types, then it is clearly incorrect to label African versions of
these tales as African derivatives or analogues of European Tale Types.
Incorrect is perhaps too mild a term. More apt might be terms like
colonialism and racism and ethnocentrism. Europeans claimed not only
African peoples and lands but African cultural products as well. It is
thus ironic for Dorson to claim a European origin for "Rabbit Rides
Fox A-courting" on the basis of a Tale Type number in the Aarne-
Thompson canon when it can be empirically shown that the canon is
faulty. This is not to say that bona fide European Tale Types did not
enter Afro-American oral tradition. A good storyteller happily adds
tales from whatever sources are available. But Dorson would seem to
be in error in claiming that the body of Afro-American tales "does not
come from Africa," Some Afro-American tales surely did come from
Africa. Not only are there African/Afro-American Tale Types without
analogues in Europe, but there are Indo-African-European Tale Types
whose most probable immediate source for Afro-American versions is
Africa. Thus, I am not necessarily arguing that Aarne-Thompson Tale
Type 15, The Theft of Butter (Honey) by Playing Godfather, is either
African or European. It will take a full-fledged comparative study of

the Tale Type to determine the possible origins and paths of diffusion of the tale. What I am saying is that the Afro-American versions of the tale seem to be cognate with African versions of the tale.

The study of the relationships between African and Afro-American cultures will surely continue.[26] I for one would like to know if there is an African/Afro-American esthetic color preference for maroon, or if there is an African/Afro-American traditional type of high-pitched near-falsetto laughter. But at least in the area of folktales, we are in a position to make qualified documented assessments as to the general nature and the specific details of the African/Afro-American tale-telling tradition.

NOTES

1. Lorenzo D. Turner, "Problems Confronting the Investigator of Gullah," in *Mother Wit from the Laughing Barrel*, ed. Alan Dundes (Englewood Cliffs, N.J.: Prentice-Hall, 1973), pp. 132–33.

2. David Dalby, "Americanisms That May Once Have Been Africanisms," in *Mother Wit*, pp. 136–40. For general discussions of the African origins of Afro-American folklore, see the section "On Origins," in *Mother Wit*, pp. 65–140. On the issue of the possible influence of African linguistic idioms on Afro-American storytelling language style, see D. J. M. Muffett, "Uncle Remus Was a Hausaman?" *Southern Folklore Quarterly*, 39 (1975), 151–66.

3. Theophine Maria Campbell, "African and Afro-American Proverb Parallels," M.A. Thesis Univ. of California at Berkeley 1975, p. 76.

4. Ibid., p. 77.

5. Richard M. Dorson, *American Negro Folktales* (Greenwich: Fawcett, 1967), p. 15.

6. Richard M. Dorson, "African and Afro-American Folklore," *Journal of American Folklore*, 88 (1975), 164.

7. A. Gerber, "Uncle Remus Traced to the Old World," *Journal of American Folklore*, 6 (1893), 249; Alan Dundes, "African Tales among the North American Indians," *Southern Folklore Quarterly*, 29 (1965), 212–13.

8. Gerber, p. 250. For representative African versions of this tale, see W. H. I. Bleek, *Reinecke Fuchs in Afrika* (Weimar: Hermann Böhlau, 1870), p. 143; Maurice Delafosse, "Le Roman de l'Araignée chez le Baoulé de la Côte d'Ivorie," *Revue d'Ethnographie et des Traditions Populaires*, 1 (1920), 214–15; John H. Weeks, *Congo Life and Jungle Stories* (London: Religious Tract Society, 1921), pp. 451–53; R. S. Rattray, *Akan-Ashanti Folk Tales* (Oxford: Clarendon, 1930), p. 131; Northcote W. Thomas, *Anthropological Report on the Edo-Speaking Peoples of Nigeria* (London: Harrison, 1910), II, 25–29; Barbara K. Walker and Warren S. Walker, *Nigerian Folk*

Tales (New Brunswick, N.J.: Rutgers Univ. Press, 1961), pp. 57–58; Peter Eric Adotey Addo, *Ghana Folk Tales: Ananse Folk Stories from Africa* (New York: Exposition Press, 1968), pp. 38–39. In some versions, the interdiction is against slapping mosquitoes rather than not scratching. Cf. Motif H 1184, Task: cutting down tree without scratching for stinging insects. The trickster succeeds by describing thrusts given or received in battle or by describing different patches of color on cows. Johannes Bolte inclined towards a European origin of the tale in his note to Bertha Ilg, "Maltesische Legenden und Schwänke," *Zeitschrift des Vereins für Volkskunde*, 19 (1909), 310, n. 2, but he cites two African versions.

9. Joel Chandler Harris, *The Complete Tales of Uncle Remus* (Boston: Houghton Mifflin, 1955), pp. 535–38; Charles C. Jones, *Negro Myths from the Georgia Coast* (Boston and New York: Houghton Mifflin, 1888), p. 85. For references to African versions, see Kenneth Wendell Clarke, "A Motif-Index of the Folktales of Culture-Area V, West Africa," Diss. Indiana Univ. 1958 (cf. Motif K 1723); and Winifred Lambrecht, "A Tale Type Index for Central Africa," Diss. Univ. of California at Berkeley 1967 (cf. her Type 1162).

10. For a typical text, see Elsie Clews Parsons, "Folk-Tales Collected at Miami, Fla.," *Journal of American Folklore*, 30 (1917), 226. See also the various references listed under "Rabbit wants to be like Rooster tale" in Tristram P. Coffin, *An Analytical Index to the Journal of American Folklore* (Philadelphia: American Folklore Society, 1958), p. 358. For references to African versions, see Elsie Clews Parsons, "Folk-Tales from Students in Tuskegee Institute, Alabama," *Journal of American Folklore*, 32 (1919), 397, n. 9; Franz Boas and C. Kamba Simango, "Tales and Proverbs of the Vandau of Portuguese South Africa," *Journal of American Folklore*, 35 (1922), 180, n. 1; Erastus Ojo Arewa, "A Classification of the Folktales of the Northern East African Cattle Area by Types," Diss. Univ. of California at Berkeley 1966 (cf. his Type 1401 [4 versions]); and Lambrecht (cf. her Type 1462A).

11. Melville J. and Frances S. Herskovits, *Dahomean Narrative* (Evanston: Northwestern Univ. Press, 1958), pp. 152–154; and Susan Feldmann, *African Myths and Tales* (New York: Dell, 1963) pp. 56–68. I tend to blame Herskovits more than Feldmann for the failure to identify the tale as an African version of a European Tale Type. It seems unrealistic and unfair to criticize popularizers and anthologizers for failing to do what scholars who publish the texts in the first place should have done!

12. Gerber, pp. 350–51; Dundes, "African Tales among the North American Indians," pp. 213–14.

13. Richard M. Dorson, "Africa and the Folklorist," in *African Folklore*, ed. Richard M. Dorson (Garden City: Anchor, 1972), p. 15.

14. William Bascom, "Folklore and the Africanist," *Journal of American Folklore*, 86 (1973), 258; Richard M. Dorson, "African and Afro-American Folklore," *Journal of American Folklore*, 88 (1975), 160, n. 23.

15. Dorson, ed., *African Folklore*, pp. 388–91. It should be noted that

sometimes informants themselves may provide clues useful in determining origins or at least immediate sources of borrowing. For example, Tale 20, "Elephant and Jackal," in *American Negro Folktales* (pp. 105–06), appears to be a version of Aarne-Thompson Tale Type 58, The Crocodile Carries the Jackal, an identification not made by Dorson. According to the Type Index, the tale is found only in India. Dorson's informant begins the tale, "It was actually India, but I put it in Louisiana. . . ."

16. It is difficult to provide the full documentation necessary to point to an African origin for these Aarne-Thompson Tale Types. Each tale is a separate research problem, the solution of which would require an exhaustive search of the vast African folktale literature. However, I shall briefly indicate some of the evidence for my assertion. Tale Type 5, Biting the Foot: Even the Aarne-Thompson index notes sixteen African versions of the tale (mostly from May Augusta Klipple, "African Folk Tales with Foreign Analogues," Diss. Indiana Univ. 1938, pp. 23–31). For other versions, see Clarke (under Motif K 543, Biting the Foot) and Lambrecht (under her Type 2251). Tale Type 37, Fox as Nursemaid for Bear: The Aarne-Thompson Index shows thirty versions from Africa. For references to other texts, see Arewa and Lambrecht (under their Type 855) and Clarke (under Motif K 931, Sham nurse kills enemy's children). Tale Type 66B, Sham-dead (Hidden) Animal Betrays Self: The Aarne-Thompson Index mentions twelve versions from India and then mentions only an Uncle Remus text and occurrence in the West Indies, citing Helen Leneva Flowers, "A Classification of the Folktale of the West Indies by Types and Motifs," Diss. Indiana Univ. 1952, referring to Motif K 607.3, Sham-Dead Man Deceived into Making Gesture. (Actually, in the 1961 edition of the Aarne-Thompson Index, the Flowers Index was inadvertently not included in the initial bibliographical listing, "Abbreviations and Bibliography," which makes it almost impossible for nonfolklorists using the index to decipher or locate this valuable comparative source study. Allusions to "West Indies: Flowers" under individual Tale Types are obviously insufficient.) For African texts, see Klipple (under Motif K 607.3) and Lambrecht (under her Type 1233). It might be noted that, although the tale is not common in the New World, it does occur in Afro-American tradition, e.g., William Owens, "Folklore of the Southern Negroes," in *The Negro and His Folklore in Nineteenth-Century Periodicals*, ed. Bruce Jackson (Austin: Univ. of Texas Press, 1967), p. 151 (originally published in 1877). See also Flowers, p. 646 (item 34). More importantly, the tale is not reported in Europe. Tale Type 73, Blinding the Guard: The Aarne-Thompson Index indicates ten versions from Africa, more versions than from anywhere else except Afro-America. It is extremely rare in European tradition (cf. the distribution indicated under Motif K 621, Escape by blinding the guard). For additional African texts, see Arewa (under his Type 2057) and Clarke (under Motif K 621). See also B. A. Lewis, "Murle Folk Tales," *Sudan Notes and Records*, 28 (1947), 141–43. Tale Type 122D, "Let me Catch you Better Game": The distribution indicated under this Aarne-

Thompson Type (and under Motif K 553.1) is limited. However, it does occur in Africa and Afro-America, and it is exceedingly rare in Europe. Tale Type 126, The Sheep Chases the Wolf: The indications from the references under this Type and under Motif K 1715, Weak animal (man) makes large one (ogre) believe that he has eaten many of the large one's companions, are that the tale is widely reported in Africa and Afro-America. For some unknown reason, the half dozen or so African versions synopsized in Klipple (under Type 126*) are not cited in the Aarne-Thompson distribution summary. For another version, see Lambrecht (under her Type 1785). Tale Type 1530, Holding up the Rock: The Aarne-Thompson Index indicates eleven versions from Africa (from Klipple). For additional versions, see Arewa (under his Type 1934). There are many more versions of this tale in African and Afro-American tradition than in European.

This is by no means anything approaching a full list of possible African/ Afro-American Tale Types either within the Aarne-Thompson canon or without. There are many other possibilities. For example, consider the curious tale, "Brother Rabbit Takes a Walk" (Tale 53), in *Nights with Uncle Remus*, in which rabbit proposes to sew up dog's mouth, a tale that Gerber compared to Aarne-Thompson Tale Type 110, Belling the Cat (cf. Gerber, pp. 255–56). The tale is almost certainly related to an Afro-American tale in which rabbit alters dog's mouth so that dog will be able to whistle or sing. For texts, see Mary Walker Finley Speers, "Negro Songs and Folk-Lore," *Journal of American Folklore*, 23 (1910), 438–39; "Negro Tales from Georgia," *Journal of American Folklore*, 25 (1912), 125–26; Zora Neale Hurston, *Mules and Men* (New York: Harper & Row, 1970), pp. 139, 146. This is similar to a tale cited in Lambrecht (her Type 1516) in which a sparrow persuades a dog to have his mouth split in order to be a better singer. In both African and Afro-American versions, there is reciprocal mutilation insofar as the tale ends with the dupe biting off the trickster's tail.

It is also highly likely that formula and dilemma Tale Types can be shown to belong to an African/Afro-American tradition. For example, Aarne-Thompson Tale Type 2053A, The House the Old Man was to Build, which has Afro-American distribution, may be related to Arewa Type 4277; or Aarne-Thompson Tale Type 1655, The Profitable Exchange, may be African in view of Klipple's dozen versions. See also Arewa (his Type 4266) and Clarke (under Motif Z 47, Series of trick exchanges). As for dilemma tales, which Bascom has convincingly demonstrated constitute an important and rich component of African narrative repertoires, one might well expect to find instances in Afro-America and indeed one does. Two texts are reported, for example, in Arthur Huff Fauset, "Negro Folk Tales from the South," *Journal of American Folklore*, 40 (1927), 261–62, which involve three suitors. Both texts refer to performing a manual act in miraculously fast fashion. The tales end with a question as to which suitor was the quickest. While one text contains Motif F 665.1, Skillful barber shaves running hare, which would suggest Aarne-Thompson Tale Type 654, The Three Brothers, the emphasis upon fantastic speed is reminiscent of "Shoot Arrow through Rock" in Bascom's *African Dilemma Tales* (The Hague: Mouton, 1975), pp. 23–26 (cf. also "Cross River Smoke," pp. 20–23). Of course, the compilation of a *complete* list of African/Afro-American Tale Types would be a project appropriate for one or more doctoral dissertations!

17. Dorson, *American Negro Folktales*, p. 16. For other Afro-American versions, see Ernest W. Baughman, *Type and Motif Index of the Folktales of England and North America* (The Hague: Mouton, 1966), under Motif B 210.2, Talking animal or object refuses to talk on Demand. Discoverer is unable to prove his claims: is beaten. For references to other versions of what Clarke labeled Motif K 1162+, Dupe tricked into reporting speaking skull, is executed, see William Bascom, *Ifa Divination* (Bloomington: Indiana Univ. Press, 1969), p. 136. Incidentally, another possible African/Afro-American Tale Type is Aarne-Thompson Tale Type 1705, Talking Horse and Dog. In this tale, an individual is frightened by a talking animal, e.g., a horse. When he remarks to his dog upon the strangeness of a horse talking, he is astonished to hear the dog reply, "Yes, isn't it." The only versions cited in the Aarne-Thompson Index are from the United States, and of those seven versions in Baughman approximately half are from Afro-American tradition. (There is also an additional version in Zora Neale Hurston, *Mules and Men* [New York: Harper and Row, 1970], pp. 217–18.) Brunvand includes the tale in his classification of shaggy dog stories, drawing attention to its popularity in American Negro tradition. See Jan Harold Brunvand, "A Classification for Shaggy Dog Stories," *Journal of American Folklore*, 76 (1963), 51 (cf. B 210, The Talking Horse and Dog). The story is a distinct Tale Type (cf. Baughman's Motifs B 210.1 and B 210.2), and it is very likely African in origin. It does *not* occur in Europe, and it apparently *does* occur in Africa. See Clarke under Motif B 210.1, Person frightened by animals successively replying to his remarks, and Motif B 211.1.7, Speaking dog. Admittedly, more African texts would be needed before one could be really confident about assuming an African origin for the tale.

18. Gerhard Lindblom, *Kamba Tales of Animals* (Upsala: Appelbergs Boktryckeri Aktiebolag, 1926), pp. 43–45. Two of the five versions cited by Arewa (under his Type 550) involve an ordeal of jumping over a river.

19. T. F. Crane, "Plantation Folk-Lore," *Popular Science Monthly*, 18 (1880–81), 826. The fire-jumping ordeal is part of "Mr. Rabbit Nibbles Up the Butter," Tale 17 in *Uncle Remus: His Songs and His Sayings*. In commenting on the tale, Crane compares it with both Grimm no. 2, "The Cat and the Mouse in Partnership," and with a version in W. H. I. Bleek's *Reynard the Fox in South Africa*, suggesting that the closer parallel was to be found in Africa rather than Europe. Dorson has never commented on Crane's pioneering essay.

20. Dorson, *American Negro Folktales*, p. 79.

21. William D. Piersen, "An African Background for American Negro Folktales?" *Journal of American Folklore*, 84 (1971), 212–13; Richard M.

Dorson, "African and Afro-American Folklore," *Journal of American Folklore*, 88 (1975), 160.

22. Edwin W. Smith and Andrew Murray Dale, *The Ila-Speaking Peoples of Northern Rhodesia* (London: Macmillan, 1920), II, 378–79. The tale may well be a version of K 851, Deceptive game: burning each other.

23. Crane, "Plantation Folk-Lore," p. 828; Ellis, "Evolution in Folklore," *Popular Science Monthly*, 48 (1895–96), 97–103; Gerber, "Uncle Remus Traced to the Old World," p. 251. The pro-European, anti-African bias in conventional folklore scholarship is exemplified in the handling of this tale. Flowers summarizes several dozen versions of this popular tale but, influenced by the borrowing of the 'open sesame' password formula from Aarne-Thompson Tale Type 676, Open Sesame, she called this tale (variously labeled as Cowmeat, Inside Cow, or In Cow's belly) a subtype of Aarne-Thompson 676. (For additional West Indies texts, see Flowers, p. 646, item 26.) Actually the confusion may have arisen from Parsons's earlier discussion of the tale in which she linked Open Sesame (Aarne-Thompson 676) with Inside the Cow. See Elsie Clews Parsons, "The Provenience of Certain Negro Folk-Tales. II. The Pass-Word," *Folk-Lore*, 29 (1918), 206–18. Except for the password (which does not occur in all versions by any means) there is little more than a general overall similarity of theme between the Indo-European tale involving the theft of robbers' treasure from a mountain cave and the African/Afro-American animal tale involving the theft of meat from inside an animal. Dorson, after dutifully citing many of the Afro-American parallels to his text, ends his headnote by trying to decide between two Aarne-Thompson Tale Types. "This story clearly has closer affinities with the Thumbling-Petit Poucet complex, where the tiny hero is swallowed by a cow . . . than with Open Sesame, to which it is linked only by one stray motif" (see Dorson, *American Nego Folktales*, p. 82). The point is that this African/Afro-American Tale Type has an identity of its own, and it is neither a subtype of Aarne-Thompson 676 nor a subtype of Aarne-Thompson 700, Tom Thumb. Dorson has claimed that his superb comparative headnotes have not been properly appreciated or understood. See "African and Afro-American Folklore," p. 158. I would say rather that in some instances he has not properly appreciated the contents of his own headnotes. In this case, we have abundant evidence of the widespread distribution of a tale in Afro-America, and *close* analogues in Africa were pointed out in the last decade of the nineteenth century. No evidence is offered by Dorson to support his claim that the story "clearly" has affinities with the Thumbling-Petit Poucet complex. Instead, the evidence offered, including citation of an interesting Senegalese version, points to an African origin.

24. Dorson, *American Negro Folktales*, p. 249.

25. For Parson's consideration of the tale, see "Die Flucht auf den Baum," *Zeitschrift für Ethnologie*, 54 (1922), 1–29; for Bascom's discussion, see *Ifa Divination*, pp. 134–36.

26. I wish to thank my helpful colleagues Larry Levine of the Department

of History and Bill Bascom of the Department of Anthropology for their generous bibliographical and other assistance in the preparation of this article. Their expertise in Afro-American and African folktales, respectively, provided an indispensable resource. Any errors in the interpretation of materials mentioned in this article are, of course, my responsibility alone.

SELECTED BIBLIOGRAPHY

Bascom, William
  1973   Folklore and the Africanist. *Journal of American Folklore* 86:253–259.
Campbell, Theophine Marie
  1975   African and Afro-American Proverb Parallels. Unpublished M.A. thesis in Folklore, University of California, Berkeley.
Crane, T. F.
  1880– Plantation Folk-Lore. *Popular Science Monthly* 18:824–33. Re-
  1881   printed in Bruce Jackson, ed., *The Negro and His Folklore in Nineteenth-Century Periodicals* (Austin: American Folklore Society, 1967), pp. 157–67.
Crowley, Daniel J.
  1962   Negro Folklore: An Africanist's View. *Texas Quarterly* 5:65–71.
Dorson, Richard M.
  1967   Origins of American Negro Tales. In *American Negro Folktales* (Greenwich: Fawcett, 1967), pp. 12–18.
  1972   Africa and the Folklorist. In *African Folklore* (Garden City: Anchor, 1972), pp. 3–67.
  1975   African and Afro-American Folklore: A Reply to Bascom and Other Misguided Critics. *Journal of American Folklore* 88:151–64.
Dundes, Alan
  1965   African Tales among the North American Indians. *Southern Folklore Quarterly* 29:207–19. Reprinted in Alan Dundes, ed., *Mother Wit from the Laughing Barrel: Readings in the Interpretation of Afro-American Folklore* (Englewood Cliffs, N.J.: Prentice-Hall, 1973), pp. 114–25.
Ellis, A. B.
  1895– Evolution in Folklore: Some West African Prototypes of the Uncle
  1896   Remus Stories. *Popular Science Monthly* 48:93–104.
Garrett, Romeo B.
  1966   African Survivals in American Culture. *Journal of Negro History* 51:239–45.
Gerber, A.
  1893   Uncle Remus Traced to the Old World. *Journal of American Folklore* 6:245–57.
Herskovits, Melville J.

1941   *The Myth of the Negro Past* (New York: Harper, 1941).
Kurath, Gertrude P.
1965   African Influences on American Dance. *Focus on Dance* 3:35–40.
Lomax, Alan
1970   The Homogeneity of African-Afro-American Musical Style. In Norman E. Whitten, Jr., and John F. Szwed, eds., *Afro-American Anthropology: Contemporary Perspectives* (New York: Free Press, 1970), pp. 181–201.
Piersen, William D.
1971   An African Background for American Negro Folktales? *Journal of American Folklore* 84:204–14.
Thompson, Robert Farris
1969   African Influence on the Art of the United States. In Armstead L. Robinson, Craig C. Foster, and Donald H. Ogilvie, eds., *Black Studies in the University* (New Haven: Yale Univ. Press, 1969), pp. 122–70.
Turner, Lorenzo D.
1949   *Africanisms in the Gullah Dialect* (Chicago: Univ. of Chicago Press, 1949).
Vance, Robert Lee J.
1888   Plantation Folk-Lore. *The Open Court* 2:1029–32, 1074–76, 1092–95.
Waterman, Richard A.
1952   African Influence on the Music of the Americas. In Sol Tax, ed., *Acculturation in the Americas* (Chicago: Univ. of Chicago Press, 1952), pp. 207–18. Reprinted in Alan Dundes, ed., *Mother Wit from the Laughing Barrel*, pp. 81–94.
1963   On Flogging a Dead Horse: Lessons Learned from the Africanisms Controversy. *Ethnomusicology* 7:83–87.
Wilgus, D. K.
1959   The Negro-White Spiritual. In *Anglo-American Folksong Scholarship since 1898* (New Brunswick: Rutgers Univ. Press, 1959), pp. 344–64. Reprinted in Alan Dundes, ed., *Mother Wit from the Laughing Barrel*, pp. 67–80.

"THE RAREST THING IN THE WORLD": INDO-EUROPEAN OR AFRICAN?

Steven S. Jones

The Aarne-Thompson synopsis of Tale Type 653A, "The Rarest Thing in the World," reads as follows:

> A princess is offered to the one bringing the rarest thing in the world [Motif H355.0.1]. Three brothers set out and acquire magic objects: a telescope which shows all that is happening in the world [D1323.15], a carpet (or the like) which transports one at will [D1520.19], and an apple (or other object) which heals or resuscitates [D1500.1.5.1, E106]. With the telescope it is learned that the princess is dying or dead. With the carpet they go to her immediately and with the apple they cure or restore her to life. Dispute as to who is going to marry her [H621.1].

Traditionally, this has been considered a folktale of Indo-European conception and diffusion. However, a comprehensive listing of the geographical distribution of Type 653A, incorporating dramatic new evidence, raises serious doubts about the validity of previous assumptions concerning that tale's origin and history.[1] In an attempt to reassess "The Rarest Thing in the World," this article will (1) identify the traditional characteristics of the tale type; (2) show how, as a result of two methodological fallacies, past studies of AT 653A have usually erroneously concluded that it was a product of Indo-European culture; (3) list all presently known collected versions of the tale; and (4) propose some alternative conclusions about the tale's source.

I. THE IDENTIFICATION OF AT 653A

Before we attempt to study "The Rarest Thing in the World," we should first establish the validity of the tale as a discrete type and describe its definitive characteristics. The similarity of AT 653A to "The Four Skillful Brothers" (AT 653), "The Suitors Restore the Maiden to Life" (AT 653B), "The Three Brothers" (AT 654), and a number of other unlisted types (e.g., "The Resuscitation of the Father,"[2] "The Joint Creation of a Woman [or Man],"[3] "The Joint Creation of an Animal," and "The Resuscitation of Two Persons with Switched Heads") requires that we have a clear conception of the folktale characteristics that differentiate AT 653A from other types and anomalous versions or, in my nomenclature, idiosyncratic tellings. The salient features of AT 653A are: I. A number of suitors desire the same maiden; II. She dies or is taken ill and is resuscitated by their joint efforts through the aid of magical gifts or powers—the steps involved generally include (1) the realization of her plight, (2) the transportation of the suitors to her, and (3) her resuscitation; and III. A decision is required as to which suitor is most worthy. This account corresponds to Aarne-Thompson's description of Type 653A, but allows for variation in the actual gifts or accomplishments that are generally associated with the action of AT 653A (the clairvoyant telescope, the flying carpet, and the resuscitating apple).[4] This descriptive definition of AT 653A provides clear grounds for distinguishing it from AT 653 (which, as Bascom points out, really involves two types—I. The Father's Test of the Accomplishments of His Sons, and II. The Rescue of a Maiden) as well as from AT 654 (which involves the testing of another set of skilled progeny) and the other unlisted types.[5] Of the latter group, "The Resuscitation of the Father" and "The Joint Creation of a Woman [or Man]" are especially close to AT 653A and sometimes share similar motifs. However, as their titles suggest, the differentiating elements in the tales are apparent enough (one involves a father figure instead of a bride-to-be, the other involves the creation of the woman instead of her resuscitation) to regard them as separate types. By and large, the collected versions that I consider tend to follow consistently one of these different story lines. This study will accordingly focus on Type 653A as a demonstrably individual tale type, versions of which are unlikely to have been multiply fabricated, because of the complexity of plot and particularly of detail, and hence are quite likely to have some direct genetic relationship with one another.

II. THE SCHOLARSHIP CONCERNING AT 653A

William A. Clouston (1888) is one of the first scholars to begin to differentiate versions of AT 653A from the other closely related Tale Types.[6] For example, he notes that in some versions the damsel is ill and not in others; this turns out to be an important characteristic that distinguishes AT 653A from AT 653. Clouston, however, follows Benfy's lead (suggested by the latter's study of AT 653) and assigns Indo-European authorship to his examples of AT 653A.[7] After citing his examples of versions of both AT 653A and 653, he simplistically concludes that we "have probably the original of all these different versions in the fifth of the *Vetalapanshavinsati* (*Twenty-five Tales of a Demon*)."[8] This reasoning is an explicit demonstration of the redaction fallacy, that is, the tendency to regard written versions as ultimate

sources for oral tales and as profoundly influencing the subsequent diffusion of oral tales. Since Clouston is not the only scholar that we will
consider who is guilty of using the redaction fallacy, we would do well
to expose the weaknesses of that assumption before proceeding.

Our willingness to trust documented written sources rather than hypo-
thetical oral sources as indicators of a tale's origin is a natural result
of our scholarly bias towards the printed word, but it is a belief that
does not appear to be justified. Oral tales have existed for centuries
without (and before) writing, so there is no reason to assume that the
act of redaction would seriously affect the oral transmission of the tale
or that it would accurately reflect the cultural origin of the tale. Where
a tale was first committed to paper would probably say more about that
culture's use of writing than about the origin of that tale. The relationship between written literature and oral literature is a valid and interesting field of study that invites much work, but blithely assuming the
influence of written tradition upon oral tradition without documented
proof or extensive study of their interaction is rash and unjustified. It
leads to the kind of misleading conclusions that have plagued the study
of "The Rarest Thing in the World."

The conclusions of Willard E. Farnham (1917) are also marred by
the redaction fallacy as he also traces AT 653A back to the *Vatalapan-
shavinsati*.[9] He cites the second, fifth, sixth, and seventh tales of that
collection as representing the original versions of Indian (and perhaps
Oriental) folktales that later evolved into the larger cycle of tales he
calls *The Contending Lovers*. Farnham identified this tale cycle as including six essential types: The Caste Type, The Resuscitation Type
(basically AT 653B), The Gifts Type (AT 653A—for which he sup-
plies an impressive bibliography of versions), The Rescue Type (AT
653), The Creation Type ("The Joint Creation of a Woman"), and
The Head Type ("Resuscitation with Switched Heads"). This early
typology corresponds fairly closely to my own findings suggested earlier in the typing of AT 653A. His identification of *The Contending
Lovers* as "above all a problem tale with an indecisive ending" fore-
shadows our most recent findings, as we shall see.[10]

Dean S. Fansler (1921) collected a number of versions of AT 653A
from the Philippines and constructed his own typology of the group of
tales closely related to it; he names the cycle the "Rival Brothers."[11] His
typology is less satisfactory than Farnham's inasmuch as he only identifies four types (I. The Creation Type, II. The Rescue of a Maiden from
Death, III. The Testing of the Sons' Skills, and IV. A Combination of
III with II); this is an incomplete listing and does not distinguish between the rescues of AT 653A and those of AT 653. Fansler's notes

are quite extensive, and he gives numerous versions of the cycle, but he also falls prey to the redaction fallacy as he traces his "Rival Brothers" cycle back to the written sources of the *Vetalapanshavinsati* (Tales 22, 5, and 2), the *Panchatantra* (No. 4), the *Pentamerone* (No. 7), the *1001 Nights* (Vol. X, p. 1 ff.), and the *Tuti-namah* (No. 5), etc.[12] In locating his four types of the "Rival Brothers," Fansler assumes Indic origins for Types I and II and European origins for Types III and IV.

Elsie Clews Parsons (1933) adopts Fansler's title of the "Rival Brothers" for the cycle.[13] Although she does not engage in speculation about AT 653A and does not always distinguish citations to AT 653A from other similar types (e.g., AT 653), her work deserves mention for its helpful bibliographical references, a number of which are to African versions that are not cited by the Type Index.

Another source valuable for its bibliographical references but one that does not engage in analysis is May A. Klipple's "African Folktales with Foreign Analogues" (1938).[14] As I discovered and as Bascom points out in *African Dilemma Tales* (p. 8), four of the tales cited under 653 in her index are actually versions of 653A; the Aarne-Thompson Type Index extends this error by listing Klipple as a reference under AT 653 but not under AT 653A. Klipple's index is also worth noting as a negative example of European ethnocentricity. Her obvious concern with, and bias towards, foreign analogues (which is to say Indo-European Tale Types), which is implicit in the title, represents an ethnocentric prejudice that has hampered the successful and impartial identification of folktales worldwide.

While European ethnocentricity is more overt in Klipple's index, it has a more serious and insidious influence in Aarne-Thompson's Type Index.[15] Folklorists and other scholars familiar with Aarne-Thompson's Type Index recognize it to be a valuable reference tool that identifies popular narrative plots (patterns) common to Indo-European peoples and the lands they settled. Among other contributions, it has helped identify Type 653A and cites a number of its occurrences. However, using the Type Index fosters at least two erroneous assumptions, which are both the products of European ethnocentricity. The first is the notion that, because the Type Index presumably considers Indo-European peoples exclusively, any and all of the Tale Types identified are essentially Indo-European, either in origin, development, or diffusion. This is a seriously inaccurate impression, for, as Daniel Crowley has pointed out in "A Tabular Analysis," many tales in the Type Index do not even occur in Europe at all, and at least one-third of the types occur outside of the cultural boundaries circumscribed by Thompson.[16]

The second serious misconception to which users of the Type Index

are susceptible is the idea that the geographical listing of the distribution of a type in the Type Index represents a reasonably accurate and
complete account of the tale's occurrence. Ultimately the fault lies with
the user, but certainly he is tempted to speculate about a type's distribution on the basis of the geographical map suggested by the Aarne-
Thompson listing. What we must not forget, however, is that Aarne-
Thompson's listing represents only the smallest portion of the exposed
surface of the vast body of oral tradition worldwide, that it has an
admittedly European ethnocentric bias, and that usually (except in a
few cases where monographs have been done on a single type) it is not
sufficiently rigorous to allow deductions about the origin or history of
particular Tale Types. More thorough collection, annotation, and index-
ing of every Tale Type are required before definite answers to the
questions about European versus African contributions to the world's
(or America's) folklore can be vouchsafed. The effect of these two misleading assumptions implicit in the Type Index upon "The Rarest
Thing in the World" are readily apparent. Not only does 653A's inclusion in the Type Index improperly imply that it is a European tale,
but the fifteen versions cited as references all appear to be directly
related to European peoples, which completely misrepresents the tale's
actual distribution.

Two recent studies of "The Rarest Thing in the World" deserve
recognition for opening the doors to new scholarship on AT 653A. The
first is Daniel Crowley's article, " 'The Greatest Thing in the World'
Type 653A in Trinidad," which considers the influence of narrative
style and local tradition upon Tale Types.[17] It carefully considers one
narrator's treatment of AT 653A and analyzes his personal stylizing
and localizing of the tale.

The second work is William Bascom's *African Dilemma Tales*, which
contains the dramatic new evidence referred to in my introduction.
Bascom has found 449 African versions (in 168 different types) of a
form of folk narrative he has termed the dilemma tale. That it is a popular form of indigenous African folklore seems reasonably demonstrated;
the startling evidence is that "actually, AT 653A is the most common
dilemma tale in Africa, with thirty-seven examples noted (36: 1–
37)."[18] A Tale Type which for years was studied from the Philippines
to Puerto Rico, from the Cape Verde Islands to Iceland, and which has
generally been considered the product of Indo-European creation and
literary diffusion turns out to be more popular in Africa than in the
countries whose natives can read the language in which the tale was
supposedly initially created and redacted. This seems to be a clear example of the weaknesses of the redaction fallacy and European ethnocen-

tricity. It is worth noting the similarity to AT 653A (either overt or structural) of many of the other dilemma tales in Bascom's collection (e.g., Tales No. 1: 1–14; 7: 1; 8: 1; 37: 1–3; 38: 1–7; 39: 1–4; 40: 1–2; 41: 1–11; 42: 1–6; 123: 1–3; 125: 1–2; and 167: 1).[19] Perusing Bascom's collection of tales makes it clear that AT 653A is no interloper; rather, we discover that AT 653A is an integral part of that widespread cultural tradition. Before we draw any further conclusions about AT 653A, let us consider the geographical distribution of the presently known, collected versions of it.

III. THE GEOGRAPHICAL DISTRIBUTION OF AT 653A

(For full citation, consult references indicated in parentheses)

Europe

> Belgium—2 (Meyer, Maurits, *Le Conte Populaire Flamand* [Helsinki: Folklore Fellows Communications No. 203, 1968])
> Bohemia—1 (Fansler)
> Greece—1 (Fansler)
> Gypsy—1 (Farnham)
> Hungary—3 (Farnham 2 and Aarne-Thompson 1)
> Iceland—4 (Farnham 3 and Aarne-Thompson 1)
> Italy—2 (Farnham)
> France—3 (Delareu, P., *Le Conte Populaire Français* [Paris: Editions Erasme, 1957])
> Poland—1 (Aarne-Thompson)
> Portugal—1 (Farnham)
> Russia—1 Fansler)
> Serbia—1 (Fansler)
> Serbocroatia—2 (Aarne-Thompson)
> Slav—2 (Farnham)
> Spain—2 (Boggs, R. S., *Index of Spanish Folktales* [Helsinki: Folklore Fellows Communications No. 90, 1930)])

Americas

> Guadeloupe—1 (Parsons)
> Dominican Republic—1 (Hansen, T. L., *The Types of the Folktale in Cuba, Puerto Rico*, etc. [Berkeley: University of California Press, 1957])
> Mexico—7 (Robe, Stanley, *Index of Mexican Folktales* [Berkeley: University of California Press, 1973])

New Mexico—4   (Aarne-Thompson apparently cite Hansen erroneously)
Nova Scotia—1   (Fauset, A. H., *Folklore from Nova Scotia* [New York: The American Folklore Society, G. E. Stechert & Co., 1931])
Puerto Rico—1   (Hansen)
Trinidad—1   (Crowley)

Other Areas

Arabia—1   (Farnham)
Iran—1   (Farnham)
Israel—8   (Jason, Heda, "Types of Jewish-Oriental Oral Tales," *Fabula* 7)
Philippines—1   (Fansler)
Turkey—1   (Farnham)

Africa (All references are to Bascom)

Adangme—1   Ghana
Akan—1   Ghana
Ashanti—2   Ghana
Betsimisaraka—1   Malgache Rep.
Bulu—1   Cameroons
Cape Verde Islands—1   (also cited by Thompson)
Dangmeli—1   Ghana
Hanya—1   S. W. Africa
Ibibio—1   Nigeria
Kongo—1   Central Africa
Kono—1   Ivory Coast
Kpe—1   Cameroons
Kpelle—2   Liberia
Krachi—1   Ghana
Limba—1   Sierra Leone
Ngonde—1   Malawi
Nkundo—4   Zaire
Ovimbundu—1   Angola
Saho—1   Somalia
Sefwi—1   Ghana
Swahili—2   East Africa
Tanga—1   Cameroons
Tanzania—1   East Africa
Temne—1   Liberia
Tsonga—1   South Africa

Vai—2   Liberia
Wala—1   Ghana
Wolof—1   Senegal and Gambia
Yao—1   Mozambique
Zigula—1   Tanzania

There are four other African versions of AT 653A in addition to Bascom's comprehensive list of thirty-seven.[20] Since the publication of his book, Bascom himself has found two more examples from North Africa and the Dan of the Ivory Coast.[21] The other two examples are:

Swahili—1   (Velten, Carl, *Märchen und Erzählungen der Sua-heli* [Berlin: W. Spemann, 1898])
Vandau—1   (Boas, Franz, and C. Simango, "Tales and Proverbs of the Vandau of Portuguese South Africa," *Journal of American Folklore*, 35 [1922])

IV.   CONCLUSIONS

It is apparent from the geographical distribution of AT 653A that we cannot simply identify it as the product of Indo-European culture. Although most of our African versions come from ethnic groups that have had considerable contact with Western peoples (as we might expect), for two reasons we cannot necessarily assume that the Africans learned the tale from the Westerners. First of all, many of the major Western peoples who had contact with Africa (for example, the English, the Germans, and the Dutch) have no versions of AT 653A themselves. Secondly, the extensive and widespread popularity of AT 653A in Africa and its presence as an integral part of a larger folk narrative tradition of dilemma tales suggest it is not a late intruder into the verbal art of Africa.

On the other hand, proponents of the Indo-European origins theory might point out the presence in Type 653A of objects that are the fairly recent products of Western culture, for example, the telescope, mirror, telephone, and flying machine that are occasionally employed as motifs in the story. However, the ability of a traditional tale to adopt new motifs is well documented, and it would seem logical that the apparently magical and impressive products of Western technology might find their way into versions of AT 653A told by African peoples who have come in contact with Westerners. In this regard, versions without apparent Western influence (of which there are a number in Bascom) and the more prototypical AT 653B in which the action is more generic and less stylized (dreaming about the problem and tracking it down as opposed to hearing about it on a telephone and flying to it in an airplane) become significant as possible examples of early versions of AT 653A and as refutations of the theory of European diffusion.

The alternative case for Westerners and other Indo-European peoples having recently (within the last two or three hundred years) learned the tale from Africans is not entirely convincing either. The European and other versions are too widespread to assume that the tale simply diffused outwards from Africa. The Indic examples of AT 653B and the Filipino and Icelandic versions of AT 653A are especially puzzling in this light.

What appears to be the most satisfactory answer to the origin of AT 653A is the proposal that, as an essential narrative pattern, its history may extend back over three or four thousand years. In essence this suggests that AT 653A is a prehistorical tale known both to Africans and Indo-Europeans that became a part of both their folkloristic heritages. This conclusion demonstrates the ultimate limitations of origins scholarship when trying to identify the authorship of possibly prehistorical tales.

Finally, the recently collected versions of AT 653A in the New World land right in the middle of the hotly debated question of African versus European contribution to New World folklore. Unfortunately, both the competing theories as to Hispanic or African diffusion of the tale to the New World appear to have some validity, so we cannot arrive at a simple conclusion either way. Despite the apparent greater popularity of AT 653A in Africa than in Spain and the reasonable conclusion that the Spaniards learned the tale from their close contact with the North Africans, we cannot dismiss the possibility that once the Spaniards learned the tale they carried it with them to the New World. Correspondingly, we must accept the extreme likelihood that the Africans would have brought this tale with them to the Americas. The popularity of the tale in the New World among Spanish-speaking peoples and among Blacks appears reasonably well documented, so that all we can conclude is that either people is likely to have brought it here. As is usually the case in the humanistic study of folklore, we are not granted simple solutions to the scholarly riddles we encounter.

NOTES

1. See William R. Bascom, *African Dilemma Tales* (The Hague: Mouton, 1975). I am indebted to Professor Bascom for generously sharing this

text with me before publication and for his opinions regarding the questions posed by this paper.

2. See Bascom, Tales No. 42: 1–6.

3. This is the middle portion of AT 945 but is also a type on its own.

4. This suggests to me the possibility that the simple action of AT 653B "The Suitors Restore the Maiden to Life" (which duplicates that of AT 653A but without the decorative motifs and which incidentally has been collected in Africa [see Bascom, Tales No. 41: 1–11, "Where is Father"] and the New World [see Elsie Clews Parsons, *Folklore of the Sea Islands, South Carolina* (Chicago: Afro-Am Press, 1969), Tale No. 66 (I, II and III), pp. 75 ff.]) may be a prototypical version of the more stylized AT 653A. Many of these tales resemble AT 653A in the same way that AT 653B does; that is, a joint resuscitation is accomplished but without the stylized motif set of magic clairvoyance, transportation, and resuscitation. Instead, many of the accomplishments tend to be quotidian (e.g., dreaming, tracking, making dinner, etc.).

5. Bascom, "Introduction," p. 7.

6. William A. Clouston, *Popular Tales and Fictions* (London, 1888), II, 281–88. Aarne-Thompson does not take this step until the 1964 revision.

7. Theodor P. Benfy, *Das Märchen von den "Menschen mit den wunderbaren Eigenschaften" seine Quelle und seine Verbreitung, Ausland*, XLI (1858), pp. 969 ff. Essentially a study of AT 653 and its migration from Orient to Occident, Benfy's work, like Clouston's and Fansler's, does not separate AT 653 and 653A.

8. Clouston, p. 285.

9. Willard E. Farnham, *The Sources of Chaucer's "Parlement of Fowles"* (Cambridge, Mass.: The Modern Language Association of America, 1917), pp. 492–518 (also published in *PMLA*, 32 [1917], 502–13). See also Farnham, "The Contending Lovers," *PMLA*, 35 (1920), 246–323.

10. Farnham, *Sources*, pp. 15–16. In his later article, Farnham does not distinguish between the resuscitations of The Gifts Type and those of AT 653B. I think it is worth distinguishing AT 653B as separate from 653A, but Farnham's identification of them as essentially the same seems to stem from the same reasons that I consider 653B to be a prototypical version of 653A. In his later study, Farnham also identifies "a few highly interesting tales from Africa" (p. 287) as versions of The Gifts Type, again foreshadowing our conclusions.

11. Dean S. Fansler, *Filipino Popular Tales* (New York: The American Folklore Society, 1921), pp. 116–37.

12. Ibid., pp. 127–37.

13. Elsie Clews Parsons, *Folklore of the Antilles, French and English* (New York: American Folklore Society, G. E. Stetchert & Co., 1933–43), vol. 3, p. 140; and *Folklore from the Cape Verde Islands* (New York: American Folklore Society, 1923), pp. 110–13.

14. May A. Klipple, "African Folktales with Foreign Analogues," Diss. Indiana Univ. 1938.

15. Antti Aarne and Stith Thompson, *The Types of the Folktale: A Classification and Bibliography* (Helsinki: Soumalainen Tiedeakatemia, 1961).

16. Daniel Crowley, "Extra-European Folktale Areas of the World: A Tabular Analysis," *Folklore Students Association Preprint Series*, July 1973; to be published in a forthcoming issue of the *Journal of the Folklore Institute*.

17. Crowley, " 'The Greatest Thing in the World' Type 653A in Trinidad," to be published in a *Festschrift* for R. Dorson.

18. Bascom, p. 7.

19. Also, there are a number of versions of "The Joint Creation of a Woman" (e.g., in Tales No. 122: 1–2 and 124:1–2), which is the middle portion of AT 945 and which I call Type *653C.

20. At least fifteen of these African versions were referenced by scholars other than Bascom (Klipple, Farnham, Parsons, Flowers, etc.) before the 1964 revision of the Type Index. This serious omission by the Type Index reveals its inherent limitations and general ethnocentricity.

21. In addition to these, Hassan El-Shamy of the Folklore Institute, Indiana University, indicated in a personal communication to Daniel Crowley (Conference on African Oral Literature, Los Angeles, 2 February 1976) that he was aware of twenty-three examples of 653A from North Africa. I am indebted to Prof. Crowley for this information as well as for the identification of the geographical location of the African examples.

AFTER THE MYTH: STUDYING
AFRO-AMERICAN CULTURAL PATTERNS
IN THE PLANTATION LITERATURE

John F. Szwed and Roger D. Abrahams

The difficulty of describing the cultural relationships between Afro-American peoples and their African progenitors is not due to any lack of data. Any argument about culture-flow is difficult to present, and needs as much ethnographic bolstering as possible, but the problems of describing the forced dispersal of African peoples in the New World is made all the more difficult because of the inadequacy of the models of culture contact and resultant change which have been used to explain such diaspora situations. Although many other massive movements of peoples have occurred analogous to the confrontation of Europeans and Africans in the New World, no clear statement exists of the variables that operate in such situations. Instead, a casual, anecdotal approach has been taken in which the encounter is seen from the viewpoint of the politically or economically superordinate people as against the subordinate, with the assumption that such subordination leads to cultural as well as political and economic dominance.

No case undercuts this model of acculturation so clearly as that of Afro-American peoples, because many of the most basic features of plantation and modern New World life have been obviously influenced by Afro-American cultural practices. Subordination was asserted and rationalized through an entirely false stereotypical concept of the slaves' cultural resources. For instance, the Africans often possessed a more highly developed agricultural technology than the Europeans, especially in tropical gardening, so that the Europeans often found themselves in an environment more alien than did their slaves. The planters not only had to exploit the physical energy source of the Africans, but also cultural practices from Africa as well as those brought from Europe, or developed subsequent to their arrival in the New World.

The planters found it convenient not only to allow African practices but actually to encourage them, especially in such noninstitutional dimensions of culture as work practices, ways of playing, and systems of magic and curing. These could be encouraged because they assisted directly or indirectly in the maintenance of the plantation and could be accommodated within the stereotypical concept of Blacks as perpetual children or as animals. In this context, active and self-conscious decul-

turation was used only to break down residual African modes of assert-
ing community because of their potential power. Thus, the various Old
World types of extended families were indeed discouraged, as were the
larger economic, political, and social units of African society. From our
perspective, desocietalization rather than deculturation resulted, and
even here total brainwashing could not have occurred.

Wherever Afro-Americans could interact with each other (whether
or not in the presence of Euro-Americans), shared expectations, attitudes, and feelings emerged drawing upon the commonalities of past
experience in Africa and in the New World. Wholesale carryovers of
community-based culture need not be posited to argue that African
cultural continuities are obvious and long-lasting. Many Euro-American
observers recognized this cultural persistence from the earliest plantation days, and provided a large, if selective, record of African and
Afro-American cultural practices as filtered through their stereotypical
rationalizations. We will look, then, at Afro-American life through the
documents of the planters and European travelers.

In *African Civilizations in the New World*, Roger Bastide states that,
"The current vogue for the study of African civilizations in America is
a comparatively recent phenomenon. Before the abolition of slavery such
a thing was inconceivable, since up till then the Negro had simply
been regarded as a source of labour, not as the bearer of a culture."
Afro-American communities could not be studied in a methodical and
holistic manner, because the techniques for analysis of cultural continuities and discontinuities are comparatively recent developments. But
whether or not Afro-Americans have such a thing as culture, an ongoing
debate on this issue dates back at least two centuries.

To anthropologists, the idea that a group could be forcibly divested
of their culture, yet maintain themselves and even proliferate, seems a
strange argument indeed. Yet this deculturation argument is still an
article of faith for most scholars studying Afro-Americans. Perhaps
Euro-Americans are still unwilling to consider the ways of Black peoples as authentic manifestations of culture unless these ways are close
enough to European practice to appear as misunderstandings or corrup-
tions. The deculturation argument, an unexamined set of assumptions,
was applied equally to other immigrant groups under the control of
capitalist economics. Their loss of culture, it is implied, happens to all
traditional peoples when they are forced off the land in search of wages.
This divestment provided the *raison d'être* of sociological study and
appears as a constant rationalizing thread of argument from Tönnies
and Durkheim through Parsons and Merton even to Frederick Barth.
This is not to say that anthropologists have been blameless in their

treatment of "the dispossessed." Redfield's folk-urban continuum is an obvious extension of Tönnies' *Gesselschaft-Gemeinschaft* distinction, and Oscar Lewis's conception of a "culture of poverty" is directly related to such "negative pastoral" arguments as are found in Durkheim and Marx, for the pastoral is the literary castigation of city-life while extolling simple country existence (cf. Williams, 1973).

THE "AFRICANISMS" CONTROVERSY

The most frustrating line of argument against the distinct features of Afro-American cultures arose in response to the work of Melville Herskovits. In 1941 in *The Myth of the Negro Past*, Herskovits listed many possible projects investigating the cultural relationships between Africans and Afro-Americans, and in the process gave a barrage of illustrations of "Africanisms." At that time the idea that American Blacks might be culturally distinct was widely rejected, and two types of counterarguments arose. On the one hand, specific Africanisms were postulated, debated, and largely rejected, a classic baby and bathwater problem. On the other, some scholars demanded that the putative African elements be demonstrated as retained from a specific African ethnic group. The Africanness of traits was not so much rejected as ignored as being incapable of adequate testing.

The frustrations of defending the cultural continuities argument have not diminished since the famous Melville Herskovits–E. Franklin Frazier confrontation after the publication of *The Myth of the Negro Past*. The basic lines of argument have not altered very much since the early 1940s, as Afro-Americanists have found to their sorrow. The following recorded conversation between Frazier and Herskovits catches the direction of the arguments and the sense of frustration:

> *Mr. Frazier*: I have not found anyone who could show any evidence of survival of African social organization in this country. I may cite a concrete case. You will recall that in reviewing my book, *The Negro Family in the United States*, in the *Nation*, you said that the description I gave of the reunion of a Negro family group could, with the change of a few words, be regarded as a description of a West African institution. But it also happens to be equally adequate as a description of a Pennsylvania Dutch family reunion. What are we to do in a case like that? Are we to say that it is African?
>
> *Mr. Herskovits*: Methodologically, it seems to me that if in studying a family whose ancestry in part, at least, came from Africa I found that something they do resembles a very deep-seated African custom, I should not look to Pennsylvania Dutch folk, with

whom this family has not been in contact, for an explanation of such a custom. I may be wrong but that seems elementary.

Mr. Frazier: But where did the Pennsylvania Dutch get their custom that resembles the one I described? Did they get it from Africa too?

Mr. Herskovits: May I ask if the methodological point at issue is this: is it maintained that if we find anything done by Negroes in this country that resembles anything done in Europe, we must therefore conclude that the Negroes behavior is derived from the European customs, the inference then being that the traditions of their African ancestors were not strong enough to stand against the impact of European ways?

Mr. Frazier: No I wouldn't say that, but I believe it should be the aim of the scholar to establish an unmistakable historical connection between the African background and present behavior of Negroes, rather than to rely on *a priori* arguments.

Mr. Herskovits: We will be in agreement, if you will add to your statement that neither should the scholar deny any such connection on *a priori* grounds. (Herskovits, 1941b:85)

Even when such arguments emerge today among social scientists, M. G. Smith's 1960 call for the tracing of specific cultural practices to a specific ethnic group in Africa is still heard; never mind that highly cognate forms of behavior exist between West Africa and the New World. There is considerable evidence of direct and specific retentions. Sea Island basketry, for instance, can be shown to be made with the same techniques and similar materials to those from Senegambia (Thompson, 1969:139–40; Perdue, 1968). Similarly, Bascom has surveyed the wide range of retentions of Yoruba and Dahomean deity-names in such New World cult religions as *Vodû, Candomblé,* and *Shango,* even while he demonstrates why such continuities have been maintained in so many culturally distinct parts of the New World (Bascom, 1972). Many other practices still to be observed in Afro-America, such as dancing, drumming, and funeral rituals, are obviously close to African antecedents.

However, Richard Price has noted that there is greater potential in seeking such "development within historically related and overlapping sets of . . . ideas" than in restricting our search to "direct retentions or survivals" (Price, 1970:375). Or as two students of Herskovits, George E. Simpson and Peter Hammond, commented:

Both past records and an examination of the contemporary situation in the New World indicate that beneath the relatively superficial level of form there is a significant, non-conscious level of psychological function. On this level there is an important basic similarity [for instance] between varieties of religious practices both throughout West Africa and in the various New World Negro communities. (Simpson and Hammond, 1960:48)

In their subsequent discussion of spirit possession, they account for its cultural tenacity through its basic commonality with West African religious behavior. Finally, rejecting M. G. Smith's assertion that continuities can only be established through commonality of form from one specific place in the Old World to one in the New, Simpson and Hammond state that:

> Form is the most superficial level of cultural reality. Since it is consciously realized, it is often much quicker to change than the profounder philosophic principles and psychological attitudes which are frequently more persistent and tenacious because they exist beneath the level of consciousness. (Simpson and Hammond, 1960:50)

But such opinions are all too rarely encountered in Afro-American scholarship. Though less strident than E. Franklin Frazer or M. G. Smith, a number of recent commentators maintain the deculturation argument while carrying out some impressive ethnographic reporting. Diverting attention from African continuities in the New World and the professed intent of the slavers to strip the slaves culturally, these scholars argue rather that if there are New World Negro cultures, they must arise for the most part from the common experiences by Blacks of enslavement and social exclusion. For example, Sidney Mintz (1970) argues that

> enslaved Africans were quite systematically prevented . . . with few exceptions . . . from bringing with them the personnel who maintained their homeland institutions; the complex social structures of the ancestral societies, with their kings and courts, guilds and cult-groups, markets and armies were not, and could not be transferred. Cultures are linked as continuing patterns of and for behavior to such social groupings; since the groupings themselves could not be maintained or readily reconstituted, the capacities of random representatives of these societies to perpetuate or to recreate the cultural contents of the past were seriously impaired. Again, the slaves were not usually able to regroup themselves in the New World settings in terms of their origins; the cultural heterogeneity of any slave group normally meant that what was shared culturally was likely to be minimal . . . [However,] the slaves could and did create viable patterns of life, for which their pasts were pools of available symbolic and material resources.

Certainly African institutions were vulnerable to elimination in the

New World, at least where they were incompatible with slavery. Still, too much contrary evidence exists for one to accept Mintz's argument without some real qualifications. One thinks, for instance, of the widespread West African practice of *susu* ("sharing group"), which has not only been encountered under the very name in several places in Afro-America, but which provides insight into the importance of such Afro-American voluntary associations as Friendly Societies, lodges, burial societies, rent parties, and the like (Crowley, 1953; Bascom, 1941; Reid, 1927). The religious domain, too, continued in modified form in a variety of cults in Brazil, Cuba, and elsewhere (Landes, 1971:1310; Herskovits, 1955; Cabrera, 1968; Bascom, 1952). Numerous expressions of apparent African nationalities occur in such festivals as the Nation Dances of Carriacou (Smith, 1962), "the dance in Place Congo" in New Orleans (Latrobe, 1951), the "jubilee" in Washington Square in eighteenth-century Philadelphia (Watson, 1857: II, 261) and many other places. Admittedly the intricate African kingship organizations could not be widely maintained in the Americas, but the relatively independent and complementary position of men and women widely observed in the slaving areas of Africa must be considered a formative force in the development of the "matrifocal" household system (Herskovits, 1941:167–86). This is what we mean by the deeper forms of culture that seem to bind Afro-Americans together.

EXPRESSIVE CONTINUITIES

Just such expressive continuities are crucial to an understanding of the institutions developed by Blacks in their various New World situations. The great diversity of New World settings in which Africans found themselves—plantations, cities, mining areas, escaped slave outposts, etc.—makes it impossible to demonstrate parallel developments in such areas as religious practice, community governance, economics, and even the family, simply in terms of the shared experiences of plantation slavery. These similarities reflect a common conceptual and affective system of which the slave could not be stripped—shared practices, beliefs, and behavioral patterns that not only survived but were developed further in the New World setting. The importance of performance in the stylization of individual and group relationships cannot be overemphasized. These patterns of performance of simplified models of social organization in the Old World provided the basic groundwork on which African-like community interactions would be generated in spite of the loss of the details of their institutional renderings.

If one uses only the literature of white journalist and traveler, the area of Black life most fully documented for continuities from the African past would be folk beliefs and practices and ghost lore. In the United States under the name of "hants," "hags," "rootwork," "conjuring," or "hoodoo," and in the West Indies as "duppies," "jumbies" (among many others) and "obeah men" or "wanga," accounts of plantation life include large sections devoted to the depth and persistence of such "superstitious" beliefs and practices.

The reasons for this interest are various. Most obvious, such practices were evidence for maintaining the stereotype of Blacks either as simpleminded heathen nature-worshipers or—even worse—as pawns of the devil. But each observer had different reasons why this subject was of interest. For the planters, these practices were seen as a threat to their operation, and they tried to militate sporadically against them, though one suspects that the folk medical practices and ceremonies were encouraged or overlooked as a way of keeping the slaves alive and happy. For abolitionists or their foes, the strange practices were proof of the presence or absence of human feeling and culture; for missionaries, they provided evidences of what had to be fought.

For whatsoever reason the observations were made, they form a large body of data that has not yet been utilized effectively in the study of cultural continuities.

Two other aspects of plantation literature of even greater interest—the materials on work and on play—will be surveyed to show the complexity of the sociocultural situation wherever African ways were transformed into Afro-American ways.

WORK

As noted, the Africans brought to the New World were often master tropical gardeners. The journal-keepers noted again and again the remarkable abilities of the slaves not only in working the cane fields and melting-houses, but also in providing their own foodstuffs even to the point of marketing the excess on their one day off, Sunday. John Luffman's account of Antigua life of 1788 is typical of such often begrudging descriptions:

> . . . every slave on a plantation, whether male or female, when they attained their 14th or 15th year, has a piece of ground, from twenty five, to thirty feet square, alloted to them, which by some is industriously and advantageously cultivated, and by others totally neglected. These patches are found to be of material benefit to the country, their produce principally supplying the "sunday market" . . . with vegetables. They are also allowed to raise pigs,

goats, and fowls, and it is by their attention to these articles, that whites are prevented from starving, during such times of the year as vessels cannot come to these coasts with safety. (pp. 94–95)

Although the contribution of the slaves to the development and operation of the plantation is yet to be studied extensively, suggestive work has been done by Peter H. Wood (1975) on South Carolina, where he shows Africans to be the source of rice agriculture, new forms of cattle breeding and herding, boat building, inland water navigation, hunting and trapping, medicine, and other skills. Indeed, the agricultural success of South Carolina seems more a function of the slaves' knowledge and technology than it was of their masters'.

The slaves often found themselves in a position to teach their masters and to carry out their agricultural tasks in agricultural time or tempo. Numerous European observers recount with amazement the coordination of activities in Afro-American work gangs, and recorded the songs sung while carrying out the work tasks. "Their different instruments of husbandry, particularly their gleaming hoes, when uplifted to the sun, and which, particularly, when they are digging cane-holes, they frequently raise all together, and in as exact time as can be observed, in a well-conducted orchestra, in the bowing of the fiddles, occasion the light to break in momentary flashes around them" (Beckford, 1790:225). Observers noted that this work was carried out through the use of songs in classic African call-and-response pattern, by which the work gangs both coordinated movements and created and maintained a sense of common purpose. Such descriptions as this, from J. B. Moreton's *West Indian Customs and Manners* (1793), are a commonplace of the genre:

> When working, though at the hardest labour, they are commonly singing; and though their songs have neither rime nor measure, yet many are witty and pathetic. I have often laughed heartily, and have been as often struck with deep melancholy at their songs:— for instance, when singing of the overseer's barbarity to them:
>
> Tink dere is a God in a top,
> No use we ill, Obisha!
> Me no horse, me no mare, me no mule,
> No use me ill, Obisha.

Such activities, of course, were given as indications that the slaves were a happy, childlike people who loved their work. As one especially lighthearted observer describes it, the harvest provided "a scene of animation and cheerfulness" in which the ear and the eye are suffused with evidences of "the light-hearted hilarity of the negroes" in which "the confused clamor of voices in dialogue and song, present a singular contrast to the calm response which nature seems to claim for herself in these clear and ardent climes" (Wentworth, 1834:I, 66).

However, it was not just the working styles that made Africans the ideal slaves in the plantation system. As a gardening people, they already measured time and apportioned energy by the cycles of the crops. They understood the necessity of working long and hard hours during planting and harvesting seasons, but they were also used to working considerably less hard during the other seasons. This disparity was often noticed, but without much comprehension of the system of time and energy allocation that lay behind it (Genovese, 1974).

From the perspective of racial stereotyping, this cycle was particularly convenient. When the Blacks were working very hard in the sun or in the heat of the building where the sugar was boiled, they could be portrayed as brute work animals. But during other seasons, when they resisted what they regarded as senseless work, they could be accused of being lazy. One way or another, the stereotype could be applied.

PLAY

Continuities of African work practices are, then, relatively easily accounted for since they fit the needs of the planters while in no way challenging the European image of Blacks. The aspect of play is more problematic because of a longer history of Black-White relations and imaginings involving a range of behaviors viewed by some as anathema to enterprise. For centuries before colonization, Europeans had associated Africans with festival entertainments; and music, dance, and public performances were ideal opportunities to judge whether or not Blacks might acquire culture. The existence of a great many detailed descriptions of Black play activities enables us to explore the deeper levels of cultural continuity, and may thus help in understanding the creation of Afro-American culture. Play materials tell us about patterns of behavior going far beyond the realm of play, for playing involves a selective stylization of motives also found in other domains of activity. For instance, Alan Lomax and associates' studies in choreometrics (Lomax, 1968) have demonstrated high correlation between work and dance movements within specific groups and culture areas. Equally important, however, in discovering deeper cultural patterns is how and to what play activities are contrasted.

Even before there was direct contact between Europeans and Africans, Black peoples from the south held a special symbolic importance for Europeans. As Henri Baudet (1965) pointed out, this interest was occasioned by a pre-Rousseauvian primitivism that included all non-Europeans, who were envisaged as simpler people living closer to nature, and therefore closer to a state of primal innocence and harmony. As travel increased, Black Africans were contrasted positively with the Muslim who had become a feared enemy during the Crusades.

However, with the beginning of the Renaissance, Europeans became more knowledgeable about Muslims and came to admire them and their culture. Baudet describes the consequences of this change:

> Unlucky Negro: our culture has always presented him in unequivocal opposition to the Muslim. But now, quite suddenly, Islam is found to merit admiration. Rapidly and unexpectedly, its star moves into a new orbit and the traditional contrast between Negro and Muslim is reversed. For a century or more Islam, and not the Negro, has been the subject of scientific interest. . . . A new reputation for the unfortunate Negro has its origins here, and he approaches the next two centuries as typifying the lowest stage of human development . . . an altogether inferior creature, a slave by nature, lacking all historical background. (p. 47)

Of course, during these "next two centuries" Africans and Europeans were brought together in huge numbers, at a time when the negative image of the primitive was convenient for rationalizing enslavement. However, during the earlier period, the fascination with Africans had caused Europeans to associate "Moors," "Blacks," and "Negroes" with parades and other kinds of festival behaviors. Eldred D. Jones's *The Elizabethan Image of Africa* (1971) brings together a number of illustrations of this fascination: blackface characters identified with Africa appeared in medieval mummers plays or in the courtly "disguises" of the sixteenth century; Henry VIII and the Earl of Essex marched with such "Moors" in 1510; blackface figures led the pageants and cleared away crowds during the same period; Edward VI took part in a Shrovetide masque in 1548 in which the marchers' legs, arms, and faces were all blackened; and Queen Anne appeared as a Negro in Ben Jonson's *The Masque of Blackness*. Numerous other Elizabethan dramas—most notably *Othello*—also contained important Black roles.

Later, after the beginning of the slave trade and the increasing presence of "real" Africans in Europe, the cultural impact became even greater. For example, Black drummers were popular in European military and court bands in the late eighteenth and early nineteenth centuries (Pierpoint, 1916; Hunt, 1873:72). Their music, style of performance, and costumes had important and lasting consequences for Europeans and Euro-Americans. And though it has been recognized that African and Turkish drum corps were the inspirations for compositions by Gluck, Mozart, and Haydn, it is not so well known that the source of the "Turkish music" (seventh) variation of the "Ode to Joy" theme of Beethoven's Ninth Symphony was not Turkish drummers (Cooper, 1970:33), but more likely the African drum corps active in Germany at that time who played what was called "Turkish music" (Pierpoint, 1916:303). Surely, part of the shock value of Beethoven's last movement for Europeans lay in its images of African drums and drummers gathering with the heavenly hosts around the throne of Heaven!

This association of Blacks with public entertainments is characteristic of marginal groups who are stigmatized because of being culturally strange. One of the few roles available to outsiders in European culture is that of the performer because it does not undermine the stereotypes. Performance abilities are utilized as one of the few ways they can survive economically. For instance, among Gypsies in Europe, this performer role has been developed into an entire way of life, as it is with the Bauls in Bengal and the Arioi society in Melanesia.

In any case, Black parades and festivals were encouraged by the plantocracy and used by them on most important entertainment occasions. Such Euro-American interest and occasional participation simply gave an unofficial stamp of approval to practices that came to fill a central role in Afro-American communities throughout the New World. In Bahia, Rio de Janeiro, Havana, Port of Spain, New Orleans, and, in past times, Mexico City, Philadelphia, North Carolina, Hartford, and other cities, Afro-American carnivals, processions, and street parades have been performed annually for many years. Though such events were often dismissed by puritanical members of Euro-American societies as licentious bacchanals, they are in fact highly structured performances based on religious cults and social clubs, many of which have continuity of more than three hundred years. The characteristics of these events are well known: clubs of maskers organize around a variety of exotic themes, elect kings and queens, make banners, and focus on such special performances as stick fighting, baton twirling, and group dancing and singing on the streets and roads. In some areas, sacred and secret symbols are displayed on this day, while in others group spirit possession occurs before the clubs make their appearances. On these days groups and their symbols are moved from the privacy of *favelas* or ghetto neighborhoods where they have been part of their street life throughout the year into the public areas where Euro- and Afro-Americans come together. The significance of these events is well recognized and feared by the guardians of public order, the police, because they know these "back-street" social organizations rule their streets after dark.

Some have dismissed these arcane and "Africa"-like institutions as the results of partial and incomplete acculturation, as way stations on the road to national homogeneousness; in other words, Blacks attempting to join or parallel Euro-American festivities with whatever cultural resources they can muster. We might better take our lead from the socio-linguists who speak of multiple codes in language systems. In the case of festivals, the codes are not linguistic ones, but instead are performance rules governing musical, motor, and religious behaviors which are the legacy of a wide variety of African peoples brought to Spanish-, Portu-guese-, French-, and English-America. These Afro-American processions and carnivals might best be described as rites of passage, not between positions in single societies, but between the performance rules and social hierarchies of two different segments of single societies. These festivities exist because of the cultural dualities present in New World societies, and they have survived through the distinctions between public and private areas of urban life. During those festivities these boundaries are broken down (Marks and Szwed, 1971), and the performances become more creole, more "country," more "down home," more African as the effects of license take hold.

Certainly the organizations that give life to these Afro-American festivals in no way approximate the complex institutional arrangements that characterize West African societies, but their existence illustrates the ways in which identification with the African homeland was maintained and how this contributed to a sense of ethnicity and cultural identity in these various Afro-American societies.

Playing carnival, *JonKanoo*, and other such festivities is regarded as the most public, unrestrained, and hence backward and most African of all of Afro-American performance occasions with the possible exception of *Shango* and other religious practices. While it is easy for Euro-Americans to be carried into the spirit of such occasions, to be able to understand how very different these performances are for Afro-Americans, it is necessary to understand the world order of Black communities, especially their contrasts between *work* and *play*, and between *private* and *public*. To relegate such expressive behavior as *JonKanoo* to the periphery of culture is to ignore the centrality of interpersonal performance in Black communities, and its use as a countervailing force against enslavement. In this context, an institution-centered definition of culture must give way to a study of micro-behaviors and the larger interactional system, which provide the formal and informal rules by which these groups live on a day-to-day, minute-to-minute basis.

Basic cultural differences exist between Euro- and Afro-American attitudes and behaviors in play and work or seriousness. Since playing is a departure from everyday behaviors especially with regard to the intensity and self-consciousness of its stylization, it is crucial to note to what play is contrasted.

Play generally has been used by Euro-Americans to describe activity free from the need to be productive within the so-called real or serious world. Although this freedom to be unproductive is often confused with freedom from rule-governed constraints, the most casual observer of play knows that the opposite is true—that playing is acting in accord with a self-consciously articulated and tightly circumscribed set of rules. Although less apparent in contest-games where winning takes precedence, the rule-governed and stylistic dimension of games nonetheless remain paramount. This concept of play is apparently characteristic of all groups, not just Euro-Americans, but Euro- and Afro-Americans differ in their use of the term and in their practices.

Euro-Americans employ the term *play* primarily in contrast to *work*, and Afro-Americans use the same terms, but what is meant by them differs sharply between the two groups. In Euro-America and elsewhere in the Western world, work is what one does to distinguish oneself as an individual. One learns to work successfully by most fully employing one's individual intelligence on a presented task. One proves one's worth by one's works, as it has been voiced until recently. Play, on the other hand, is the activity by which one progressively learns how to coordinate with others. Our values emphasize that the older we get, the more we must learn the importance of "team play." In an admittedly simple rendering then, working comes to mean, as one grows up, developing one's individual abilities, while playing during the same period comes to represent the subordination of individuality in favor of coordination and cooperation with others. Work is one's most *public* set of behaviors, and play is as private as one can maintain, unless one chooses one of our two most deviant of all our acceptable roles, the entertainer or the athlete, he who plays in public. Even here, we attempt to redefine their behavior as work. Thus, the most individual of all our behaviors, work, is also the most public.

Almost exactly the reverse characterizes Afro-Americans. Work tends to be identified with family and, by extension, with home with its relative privacy. Work is learned within the home as the most important feature of extended family living, and is identified with the maintenance of the familial order of the household. Commonly under the direction of *Mama*, children learn to work from older children in the household. Work is thus defined as a cooperative activity. Conversely, play, which is used to refer primarily to performance in this context, is learned from one's peers, commonly outside the home, and comes to be *the* activity by which Afro-American individuality is asserted and maintained. Thus, *playing* or performing is associated with public places, while work begins in the home and remains a kind of private or at least guarded range of behaviors. This accounts in part for the relative lack of discussion of work by Blacks, especially in those public circumstances in which verbal playing is regarded by them as more appropriate.

The distinction parallels that between the female-dominated household world and the male street-corner way of life, in terms of the difference of orientation, activity, and value systems between female respectability and male reputation maintenance (Wilson, 1969). In the Afro-American sense of the term, *play* is not commonly practiced in the house, being more appropriate in public where masculine, crossroads, reputation-centered values may be celebrated. In this sense play means highly unruly behavior, noisy verbal dueling, and using a dramatic speaking style known in the West Indies as *talking bad* or *broken*. When the noise, unruliness, and speaking style are brought together, the result is called *nonsense* or *foolishness*, evaluative terms derived from the household values but usually accepted by the male speakers themselves. Being public and individual, playing is regarded as inappropriate in areas dominated by respectability values, especially the house (Abrahams and Bauman, 1971; Abrahams, 1972, 1976).

Undoubtedly, the term *play* is used by Afro-Americans with many of the same meanings as other speakers of English. But in Black communities in the United States and the West Indies it has developed another range of meanings that point to an important social feature of Afro-American public behavioral style. Specifically, *play* describes situations of style- and code-switching, changes that have consequences reaching far beyond mere stylistic or esthetic dimensions of culture to the assertion of value- and culture-difference in performance terms.

Although these generalizations derive from contemporary ethnographic research, old travel literature indicates that these differences have long existed, both in the use of the word "play" and in the concept of what playing is and how it should be properly carried out. As early as 1729, A. Holt mentions that the slaves in Barbados had gatherings on Sunday, "which they call their plays . . . in which their various instruments of horrid music howling and dancing about the graves of the dead, they [give] victuals and strong liquor to the souls of the deceased" (cited in Handler and Frisbie, 1972:14). Peter Marsden similarly noted in 1788, "Every Saturday night many divert themselves with dancing and singing, *which they style plays*; and notwithstanding their week's labour, continue this violent exercise all night" (p. 33; our emphasis). Such festivities were more commonly associated with the major holidays, especially Christmas. Another commentator, William Beckford, noticed:

> Some negroes will sing and dance, and some will be in a constant state of intoxication, during the whole period that their festival at Christmas shall continue; and what is more extraordinary, several of them will go ten or twelve miles to *what is called a play*, will sit up and drink all night, and yet return in time to the plantation for their work the ensuing morning (Beckford, I, 392; our emphasis)

This different approach to time, this all-night and unrestrained performance of play, seems to have most troubled these spectators, for, almost formulaically when they mention the term, they discuss its nocturnal aspects: "The dance, or play as it is sometimes called, commences about eight o'clock . . . and . . . continues to daybreak with scarcely an intermission" (De la Beche, 1846:40).

Nothing troubled the planters more than the nighttime activities of their slaves, relating to a whole group of stereotype traits such as nighttime, diablerie, and supersexuality. Every effort was made to cut down on excessive nocturnal ceremonials, night-burials and wakes, the practice of *obeah*, and, of course, these *plays*. Yet, as anyone knows who has worked in the West Indies, the high value placed on playing any celebration all night remains to the present. Whether it is a wake, Christmas, *Carnival, tea meeting*, or *thanksgiving*, a celebration that can't be sustained all night is a disgrace to the performers and the community.

The designation of these all-night performances as *plays* was only one of the Black uses for the term, possibly fastened on by whites because it departed so fully from their own usage. In *A View of Jamaica*, James Stewart gives us some glimmer of the Afro-American domain of the term when he mentions that "Plays, or dances, very frequently take place on Saturday night" and also suggests that play is their term for any licensed nonsense occasion (Stewart, 1823:269–70). Any holiday was called a *play-day* (Lewis, 1836:45, 97), as was a wake! (Scott, 1833:204).

This set of practices, although persistently defined as bad and often illegal, has been maintained and even recently intensified throughout the anglophonic West Indies. Significantly, the most licentious of these celebrations are still referred to in play terms. One "plays" wake, Carnival *mas'*, *Christmas sport*, or any of that range of performances generally termed *nonsense* or *foolishness*.

Playing, then, means the acting out of behaviors regarded as *bad*, yet which provide a means of channeling the energies of all those in the performance environment. This acceptance of a negative self-image by at least one segment of Black communities during these "licentious" occasions has been widely noted by ethnographers. Karl Reisman (1970) has pointed out the "duality of cultural patterning" between positive (usually European) forms and negative (usually old-fashioned, country, or African) forms. It is an integral part of this performance system to seek power by playing out in public these negative roles. These *bad* performances, regarded as appropriately masculine, embody male reputation values. This kind of nonsense behavior is acted upon constantly by the *sporty fellows*, *bad-johns*, and *rude boys*, but only when *playing* is sanctioned are the *sporty* ones permitted to perform before the community as a whole, and then only by dressing up or dressing down, taking unaccustomed roles into which they channel their antinormative (i.e., antihousehold) *nonsense*.

Thus *playing* in anglophonic Afro-America means not only the switching of styles and codes characteristic of all types of play, but also the switching downward to roles and behaviors regarded from household (and Euro-American) perspectives as "bad" or improper. Furthermore, as Morton Marks has noted of this switching in other parts of Afro-America, it is "always from a 'white' to a 'Black' style" and in music and dance at least, "from a European to an African one" (Marks, 1972:5). The juxtaposition of the implicitly "good" household-based norms of the Black community with the "bad" activities produces the kind of mass release of energies noted by all observers of Afro-American celebrations. *Playing* then means playing bad, playing Black, playing lower class. It is no coincidence that playing Christmas often led to insurrection, as was noted by the planter-journalists and travelers. The play world with its nonsense, masculine, defensive, and regressive Black motives simply began to break down the boundaries and rules of play, spilling out over the fences into the yards of the great houses.

Play is used in an analogous but somewhat more restricted sense in Black talk in the United States. Here *playing*, *playing the dozens*, and other similar locutions refer to code-switching into *baaad* varieties of speaking and acting which call for the same kind of performative acceptance of the negative role to obtain the power inherent in such behaviors. Thus, throughout Afro-America, playing is equated with a powerful but negative image of the performer. The power in the liminal world is a means of *getting into it*, setting up *the action*, but such play-ing provides a constant threat to the household world.

This speaking frame of reference acts both positively, in establishing the street environment as an appropriate place of witty and inverted performances, and negatively, in restricting speaking behavior within the household and other places dominated by respectability values (Abrahams, 1970). In the Afro-American order of behaviors, "play" is not distinguished from "real" or "work" but from "respectable" behavior. Play is thus conceived in a very different way in Afro-American communities than it is in Euro-American. It is an important element of public performance of Black communities, by which Black men-of-words are able to establish and maintain their "reputations." The descriptions of West Indian *plays* give an indication of the depth of interest given such entertainments. Through these accounts we can gain insight not only into the alternative attitude of playing, but also into the ambivalence of Euro-Americans to such energetic practices, and the ways in which the slaves gradually incorporated European play oc-casions and in the process developed an Afro-American Creole culture.

With *plays*, as with the performance events introduced into Afro-American life from Europe, the focus and uses of the performances were changed in accord with the ethical and esthetic conceptual system shared by Africans and Afro-Americans. This process can be better understood by reference to the "Creole language hypothesis," which seeks to demonstrate that English, French, and other New World Creole languages are all developments from a West African Creole tongue used by traders and combining Portuguese and West African features (Whinnom, 1965; Stewart, 1967, 1968; Dillard, 1972). Those who pursue this line of argument point to the large number of under-lying similarities between the various New World Creole systems ac-counting for the major differences in vocabulary by relexification, the simple substitution of a different (European) word into the phono-logical and morphological structure of the West African-based language. This word (or phrase) substitution does not necessarily mean that the vocabulary substituted is used with the same system of reference. Indeed, there is good evidence that the process of relexification cannot be understood without taking into account the *calque* (or "loan transla-tion"), words that are translated into their nearest Western equivalent, but that continue to be used in the same system of reference as in Africa. This process of vocabulary substitution has ramifications in the entire semantic realm, in joking and oratory as well as in song and dance (Abrahams, 1970a, 1972, 1976).

Whether or not the Creole language hypothesis proves valid, something like relexification seems to have operated on this larger communication level. One can observe in speech-making events throughout English-speaking Afro-America the utilization of the oratorical variety of Standard English, but in contexts that demand a different performer-audience relationship than can be found in British usage, and for purposes that are in many ways diametrically opposite to the British practices. A similar pattern holds true with song and dance, in the adaptation of the "sentimental song" and European formal dances such as quadrilles for marking formal, more respectable public occasions.

CONCLUSION

In the process of exploring Afro-American cultures through material such as these journal accounts and histories, the object should not be simply to search out "Africanisms" as survivals of African traditions but rather to use Africa as a base line, as a starting point, as in fact it was historically. The numerous Afro-American cultures of contemporary North and South America provide important points of comparison. Instead of searching out the *sources* of this or that pattern of behavior, parallel *processes* and *functions* must be searched out in Africa and Afro-America after European colonialism and slavery. As Hortense Powdermaker pointed out long ago in *After Freedom*, her study of a Mississippi community, in taking on new cultural values from the whites, the Blacks did not simply replace older "African" values, but rather added newer patterns onto older ones. This is what Paul Radin meant when he suggested that the "Negro was not converted to [the white Christian] God. He converted God to himself" (1969:ix). Both implied that African sensibilities were the starting place and that European values were selectively adapted to the specialized need of Afro-Americans. While all of this is rather elementary anthropology, in taking up the politically charged subject of the roots and nature of Afro-American culture, we must remind ourselves of the universal principles operating in the most diverse groups of the earth's peoples.

The demands of Afro-American students for a cultural history that is relevant to Black people—that is, one that considers both the past and the present of Blacks—have often been dismissed as lacking substance. Such dismissals depend entirely on the view that no unique Afro-American cultural past exists beyond that of Africa and the plantation's institutional requirements. This connection between the two is at best considered more discontinuous than continuous, and at worst nothing more than (to use Ralph Ellison's phrase) the sum of a people's brutalization.

Herskovits recognized this view for what it was, the myth of the Negro past. We would add that it also constitutes the myth of the Negro present, and it is to this myth and its debunking that we have addressed our argument here.

BIBLIOGRAPHY

Abrahams, Roger D.
1976 *Talking Black*. Rowley, Mass.: Newbury House.
1975 "Negotiating Respect: Patterns of Presentation among Black Women," *Journal of American Folklore*, 88:58–80.
1972 "Talking My Talk: Black English and Social Segmentation in Black Communities," *The Florida F/L Reporter*, 10:29–38.
1970 *Positively Black*. Englewood Cliffs, N.J.: Prentice-Hall, Inc.
1970a "Traditions of Eloquence in the West Indies," *Journal of Inter-American Studies and World Affairs*, 12:505–27.
Abrahams, Roger D., and Richard Bauman
1971 "Sense and Nonsense on St. Vincent: Speech Behavior and Decorum in a Caribbean Community," *American Anthropologist*, 73(3):262–72.
Bascom, William R.
1972 *Shango in the New World*. Austin: African and Afro-American Research Institute Occasional Publication, University of Texas.
1952 "The Focus of Cuban Santeria," *Southwestern Journal of Anthropology*, 6:64–68.
1941 "Acculturation among the Gullah Negroes," *American Anthropologist*, 43:43–50.
Bastide, Roger
1971 *African Civilization in the New World*. New York: Harper and Row.
Baudet, Henri
1965 *Paradise on Earth: Some Thoughts on European Images of Non-European Man*. New Haven: Yale University Press.
Beckford, William
1790 *A Descriptive Account of the Island of Jamaica*. London.
Cabrera, Lydia
1968 *El Monte*, 2d ed. Miami: Rema Press.
Crowley, Daniel J.
1953 "American Credit Institutions of Yoruba Type," *Man*, 53:80.
De La Beche, H. T.
1846 *Letter from the West Indies*. London.
Dillard, J. L.
1972 *Black English*. New York: Random House.
Genovese, Eugene

1974   *Roll Jordan Roll.* New York: Pantheon Books.
Handler, Jerome C., and Charlotte J. Frisbie
1972   "Aspects of Slave Life in Barbados: Music and Its Cultural Context," *Caribbean Quarterly,* 11(4):5–46.
Herskovits, Melville J.
1955   "The Social Organization of the Candomble," *Anaais do XXXI Congresso Internacional de Americanistas,* 1954, Sao Paulo, 505–32.
1941a   *The Myth of the Negro Past.* New York: Harper.
1941b   *The Interdisciplinary Aspects of Negro Studies.* Washington, D.C.: American Council of Learned Societies Bulletin No. 32.
Hunt, Leigh
1873   *Wishing Cap Papers.*
Jones, Eldred D.
1971   *The Elizabethan Image of Africa.* Charlottesville: University of Virginia Press.
Landes, Ruth
1971   Review of *Afro-American Anthropology,* eds. Norman E. Whitten, Jr., and John F. Szwed, *American Anthropologist,* 73:1306–10.
Latrobe, Benjamin Henry
1951   *Impressions Respecting New Orleans.* New York: Columbia University Press.
Lewis, M. G.
1836   *Journal of a West India Proprietor.* London.
Lomax, Alan
1968   *Folk Song Style and Culture.* Washington, D.C.: American Association for the Advancement of Science.
Luffman, John
1788   *A Brief Account of the Island of Antigua.* London.
Marks, Morton
1972   "Performance Rules and Ritual Structure in Afro-American Music." Diss. Univ. of California at Berkeley.
Marks, Morton, and John F. Szwed
1971   "Afro-American Cultures on Parade," paper read at the American Anthropological Association's Annual Meeting, New York City, 1971.
Marsden, Peter
1788   *An Account of the Island of Jamaica.* Newcastle.
Mintz, Sidney
1970   "Foreword," in *Afro-American Anthropology: Contemporary Perspectives,* ed. Norman E. Whitten, Jr., and John F. Szwed. New York: The Free Press.
Moreton, J. B.
1793   *West Indian Customs and Manners.* London.
Perdue, Robert E., Jr.
1968   "African Baskets in South Carolina," *Economic Botany,* 22:289–92.

Pierpoint, Robert
   1916   "Negro, or Coloured, Bandsmen in the Army," *Notes and Queries*,
          2:303–04.
Powdermaker, Hortense
   1939   *After Freedom: A Cultural Study in the Deep South*. New York:
          The Viking Press.
Price, Richard
   1970   "Saramaka Woodcarving: The Development of an Afro-American
          Art," *Man*, 375.
Radin, Paul
   1969   "Foreword," to *God Struck Me Dead*, ed. Clifton H. Johnson.
          Philadelphia: Pilgrim Press.
Reid, Ira De A.
   1927   "Mrs. Bailey Pays the Rent," in *Ebony and Topaz*, ed. Charles S.
          Johnson. New York: National Urban League, pp. 144–48.
Reisman, Karl
   1970   "Cultural and Linguistic Ambiguity in a West Indian Village,"
          in *Afro-American Anthropology: Contemporary Perspectives,* ed.
          Norman E. Whitten, Jr., and John F. Szwed. New York: The
          Free Press.
Scott, Michael
   1833   *Tom Cringle's Log*. Edinburgh: Blackwoods.
Simpson, George E., and Peter B. Hammond
   1960   "Discussion," in *Caribbean Studies: A Symposium*, ed. Vera Rubin.
          Seattle: University of Washington Press. pp. 46–53.
Smith, M. G.
   1962   *Kinship and Community on Carriacou*. New Haven: Yale Univer-
          sity Press.
   1960   "The African Heritage in the Caribbean," in *Caribbean Studies: A
          Symposium*, ed. Vera Rubin. Seattle: University of Washington
          Press, pp. 34–46.
Stewart, James
   1823   *A View of the Past and Present State of the Island of Jamaica*.
          London: Oliver and Boyd.
Stewart, William A.
   1968   "Continuity and Change in American Negro Dialects," *The Florida
          F/L Reporter*, 6(1):3–14.
   1967   "Sociolinguistic Factors in the History of American Negro Dialects,"
          The Florida F/L Reporter, 5(2):11–29.
Thompson, Robert Farris
   1969   "African Influence on the Art of the United States," *Black Studies
          in the University: A Symposium*, ed. Armstead L. Robinson, et al.
          New London: Yale University Press, pp. 122–70.
Watson, John F.
   1857   *Annals of Philadelphia and Pennsylvania, in the Olden Times*.
          Philadelphia: Edwin S. Stuart.

W. B. H.
  1916   "Negro, or Coloured, Bandsmen in the Army," *Notes and Queries*,
         2:378.
Wentworth, Trelawney
  1834   *A West Indian Sketch Book*. London.
Whinnom, Keith
  1965   "The Origin of European-based Creoles and Pidgins," *Orbis*, 14:
         511–26.
Williams, Raymond
  1973   *The Country and the City*. New York: Oxford University Press.
Wilson, Peter J.
  1969   "Reputation and Respectability: Suggestions for Caribbean Eth-
         nology," *Man*, 4:70–84.
Wood, Peter H.
  1975   " 'It was a Negro Taught Them,' A New Look at African Labor
         in early South Carolina," in *Discovering Afro-America*, ed. Roger
         D. Abrahams and John F. Szwed. Leiden: E. J. Brill.

THE AFRICAN CONNECTION:
Comments on *African Folklore in the New World*

Richard M. Dorson

In this stimulating volume, seven contributors present evidence for the transplantation of African culture traits and institutions to the Americas and the Caribbean. Of these essays Daniel J. Crowley, who assembled them, writes: "Together they are the latest riposte of the Africanist folklorists in their long duel with the European Diffusionists over the origins of the tales told in the New World by Black people. As such, they answer . . . Richard Dorson's 'African and Afro-American Folklore: A Reply to Bascom and Other Misguided Critics.' "[1]

In fact, only one essay deals with my thesis. The thesis is that most of my *American Negro Folktales* do not come from Africa. Crowley and Bascom, in the Herskovits tradition, speak of the New World en bloc (although Herskovits himself was very chary of identifying African retentions in the United States; I remember him saying, when I was a postdoctoral fellow at Northwestern in 1952, "I don't know what I see here"). But I have always sharply differentiated black traditions in the United States from black traditions in the rest of the New World. In *American Negro Folktales*, I wrote:

> The conclusion emerges that the New World Negro repertoire falls into two groups of stories, one pointing toward Africa and one pointing toward Europe and Anglo-America. The Atlantic and Caribbean islands and northeastern South America comprise the first block and the plantation states of the Old South the second block.[2]

Because this point escapes Dan Crowley, the examples he gives of Bascom reporting a Yoruba myth in Cuba and Steven S. Jones uncovering an African pedigree for what Dan had construed as a European tale in Trinidad do not at all, as he claims, make points for his side. Rather, they confirm my own position, because no Yoruba myths have been recorded in mainland United States, and the diaspora of Aarne-Thompson Type 653A, "The Rarest Thing in the World," that Jones so fully documents never enters the Afro-American tradition in the United States, by his own evidence. Using chiefly Bascom's data in his *African Dilemma Tales* (1975), Jones reports forty-three Pan-African versions. Yet for mainland United States he can cite only four texts from New Mexico in the Hispanic tradition. The dilemma tale is a particularly African form not current among United States blacks.

Bascom does not err as broadly as Crowley when he writes: "Some folklorists still maintain that few, if any, African folktales are known in America. While they may be referring only to the United States, they speak of America." This is an unscholarly statement, since he gives no citations to "they" and is disingenuous in saying "they speak of America." Historians of the United States call themselves American historians. Their society is the Organization of American Historians. Scholars of United States civilization belong to the American Studies Association. In my essay, "The Origin of American Negro Folktales," I distinguished between the United States and the rest of the New World, and I specifically discussed Crowley's *I Could Talk Old-Story Good: Creativity in Bahamian Folklore* as illustrating the Africanist repertory of New World blacks outside the United States in contrast to the largely non-Africanist repertory of United States blacks. I also cited Martha Warren Beckwith's *Jamaica Anansi Stories* to make the same point. Let any reader pick up Crowley or Beckwith and compare their contents with the mainland collections of Hurston, or Brewer, or Abrahams, or Dorson and it will be obvious, without recourse to type and motif indexes, that there is a vast difference between their worlds.

My larger objection to Bascom's statement is that he has given the discussion a false face. It is not that "some" folklorists still deny African origins but that current commentators continue to proclaim African origins. My grievance is directed at the continued repetition of the cliché that United States Negro folktales come from Africa, after I discovered for myself, and made the evidence available for others, that most of the thousand tales I collected in 1952 and 1953 did not come from Africa. To get the record straight, I have said and repeat that I am not a "proponent of European origins" but of "multiple origins, including the African."[3] And I speak only of oral narratives.

Now we turn to the essay by Alan Dundes on "African and Afro-American Tales." Dundes addresses himself directly to my points and uses the correct methods of analyzing tale type origins. Clearly, here is a well-trained folklorist.[4]

The essence of Dundes' argument is that the first seven, and possibly others, of my *American Negro Folktales* may come from Africa. He does not note that I have enumerated six stories, collected by Alfred B. Ellis on the Gold Coast, as variants of texts which appear in my collection and that I say "these animal tales do constitute the core of the case for African origins."⁵ They include the first tale, "Who Ate Up the Butter?" which is followed by three variants, one of which is interwoven with "The Tar Baby," also reported by Ellis. So, although Dundes speaks of Dorson's first four tales as possibly coming from Africa, he really deals only with one, which I have already stated as being probably Africa-derived. My seventh tale, "Rabbit and Bear Inside the Elephant," is also one of the parallels from Ellis that I list. This list further includes "Rabbit Rides Fox A-courting," Type 72, which Dundes discusses in some detail (and which I myself collected in Liberia), number 10 in *American Negro Folktales*; Type 1074, "Race Won by Deception," to which Dundes alludes (number 9 in *American Negro Folktales*); and "Rabbit and Bear Inside the Elephant" (number 7 in *American Negro Folktales*), which he considers a separate African tale type (see his note 23). So Dundes is not covering new ground here but elaborating on tale types I had already suggested as African.

Dundes has done good work in pursuing these potential African tale types, and there is no question that a tale should not be considered European simply because it can be located in Aarne-Thompson. But I had already indicated that the group of tales in the first half of chapter 1 "constitute the core of the case for African origins." And his leap to the conclusion that "Dorson would seem to be in error in claiming that the body of Afro-American tales 'does not come from Africa' " is demonstrably his error. First, I spoke not of *the* body but of *this* body,⁶ that is, referring to my own collection. Dundes is unhistorical in trying to generalize about "the body of Afro-American tales" since, as I had already said, the corpus of 1950 will differ from the corpus of 1850, which should contain a higher number of African tale types in active circulation than those being told at the later date.

Now I repeat my 1967 statement that "this body of tales does not come from Africa." Some may come from Africa, but most—the great majority—do not. Just look at the table of contents in *American Negro Folktales*. Fifteen chapters contain two hundred and forty-four tales. Only the first half of the first chapter, "Animal and Bird Stories," with thirty-four tales, lends itself to Africanist exegesis, as African analogues are lacking for the buzzard and poll parrot cycles. The rest of the chapters contain almost wholly Anglo-American, Euro-American, and black American traditions: the Old Marster cycle set on the plantation, witch stories duplicating farmers' tales from the Salem witchcraft trials, Irish jokes, preacher jests, ghost stories, highly localized hoodoo memorates, brutality tales of slavery and Jim Crowism, tall tales, noodle stories, biblical and devil legends, wonders of natural history, buried treasure legends. Very rarely does an African motif emerge in these nonanimal tales, such as in "Talking Bones" (tale number 50, motif B210.2, "Talking animal or object refuses to talk on demand") or, as Dundes points out, in "Rangtang" (tale number 125, motif B421, "Helpful dog"). But the vast majority of the narratives have no African connection. Tales of slave beatings, of escapes on the underground railroad, of buried Confederate money, of wonderful shooting grow directly out of life in the United States. The ghost, witch, and devil are standard English transplants. All this I have said. Dundes simply ignores 90 percent of the *American Negro Folktales*.

Since Dundes—and all the contributors to this volume—stress only the African connection, their discussion is unbalanced. Dundes makes no mention of the tales I have found to be widespread in United States Negro tradition: "The Coon in the Box" (35 in *American Negro Folktales*), best known of all Old Marster stories, based on the Indo-European motif K1956, "Sham wise man," found in the Grimms' tale Doctor Know-All; "The Mean Boss" (50), traceable to England through motif J1341.11, "Hired men sing of displeasure with food"; "The Fight" (38), between two strong slaves owned by rival planters; "The Mermaid" (126), reported only in my eight United States Negro variants; "The Flower Bed of Eve (Ease)" (64), brought into the repertory of United States blacks from an English and continental ancestry traceable, according to the examination of nearly a hundred variants by Kenneth Jackson and Edward Wilson, to an origin in Germany, where the first printed text is dated 1479; "Baby in the Crib" (41), known as the Mak story in the Second Shepherd's Play from the fifteenth century; "Brother Bill" (220), a surprise rendition of Pecos Bill as a black cowboy; "King Beast of the Forest Meets Man" (18), the most popular animal tale I encountered, with eighteen variants, Type 157, widely distributed throughout Europe but very rarely reported in Africa; "The Snake and the Baby" (145), the belief legend whose dispersion in Europe and the United States has been treated in an Indiana University doctoral dissertation; and so on and so on. Dundes and other Africanists unearth a couple of Anansi and dilemma tales from mainland United States to try to prove their currency, but the indisputable fact is that I never heard any example of either in the thousand plus tales I collected.

Dundes asks me to comment on T. F. Crane's review article of *Uncle Remus, His Songs and His Sayings*, published in *Popular Science Monthly* in 1880 under the title "Plantation Folk-Lore." In this review

Crane, a worthy pioneer American folklorist, notes European, African, and South American Indian variants to some of the Uncle Remus tales and comes down for African origins. I choose to cite the article by Alfred B. Ellis, "Evolution in Folklore: Some West African Proto-types of the Uncle Remus Stories," from *Popular Science Monthly* of 1895, as particularly pertinent to the discussion, for Ellis himself collected (as Crane did not) six tales on the Gold Coast which correspond to texts in *American Negro Folktales*. (Bruce Jackson reprints the Crane but not the Ellis article in *The Negro and His Folklore in Nineteenth-Century Periodicals*.) If we are quoting early opinions, William Owens, in his 1877 essay on "Folklore of the Southern Negroes" in *Lippincott's Magazine*, wrote of the "Foot-Race" story (Type 1074, number 9 in *American Negro Folktales*): "Substantially the same story is to be heard from the natives of each of the four continents, but whether the African gained his idea of it from Europe or Asia, or whether the European or Asian gained it from Africa, is perhaps past determining."[7]

So where do we stand on the continuing debate over the African connection? I confess to considerable disappointment that space is misused because of Crowley's and Bascom's failure to read my simply stated distinction between mainland United States and other parts of the New World. Dundes has performed a real service in pinning down a few potential African tale types, but he has overplayed his hand in claiming far more than this proposition, which I had already recognized, would justify. Ten percent still seems about the right estimate for the number of *American Negro Folktales* that reveal the African connection.

NOTES

1. My article cited by Crowley appeared in *Journal of American Folklore,* 88 (1975): 151–64.
2. Greenwich: Fawcett, 1967, p. 17; cf. "African and Afro-American Folklore," p. 163.
3. "African and Afro-American Folklore," p. 162.
4. Dundes studied at Indiana University with, among others, Dorson.—Ed.
5. "African and Afro-American Folklore," p. 157 and note 16.
6. *American Negro Folktales,* p. 15.
7. Reprinted in Bruce Jackson, ed., *The Negro and His Folklore in Nineteenth-Century Periodicals,* American Folklore Society Bibliographical and Special Series 18 (Austin: University of Texas Press, 1967), p. 151.

NOTES ON THE CONTRIBUTORS

Roger D. Abrahams is Chairman of the Department of English at the University of Texas at Austin and is currently on leave as a Fellow of the National Humanities Institute at the University of Chicago. An authority on Caribbean and Afro-American folklore and folklore theory, he is currently looking toward the Mediterranean.

William Bascom is Director of the Lowie Museum of Anthropology at the University of California, Berkeley, and a leading authority on African art, folklore, and divination, especially among the Yoruba. His current research is in identifying folktales in the United States which came from Africa.

Daniel J. Crowley is Professor of Anthropology and Art at the University of California, Davis, and has collected art and folklore in West and Central Africa and studied the Carnival of Trinidad, West Indies.

Richard M. Dorson is Distinguished Professor of History and Folklore at Indiana University and Director of its Folklore Institute. He has written and edited twenty-four books, including *African Folklore* (1972) and *Folklore and Fakelore* (1976).

Alan Dundes is Professor of Anthropology and Folklore at the University of California, Berkeley, editor of *Mother Wit from the Laughing Barrel: Readings in the Interpretation of Afro-American Folklore* (1973), and author of many papers on the subject.

Steven S. Jones is a doctoral candidate in Folklore and Literature at the University of California, Davis, in cooperation with Berkeley, and is interested in both Anglo- and Afro-American traditions.

William D. Piersen is Visiting Assistant Professor of History at Texas Technological University, Lubbock, and specializes in Caribbean and Afro-American history.

John F. Szwed is Director of the Center for Urban Ethnography and Professor of Folklore and Folklife at the University of Pennsylvania, presently working on the creolization of literatures in his ongoing study of American ethnography.

INDEX

AARNE-THOMPSON TALE TYPES[1]

4, Carrying the Sham-Sick Trickster, 41

5, Biting the Foot, 42, 45, 48

15, The Theft of Butter (Honey) by Playing Godfather, 43–45, 89

37, Fox as Nursemaid for Bear, 42

55, The Animals Build a Road (Dig Well), 42

58, The Crocodile Carries the Jackal, 48

66B, Sham-Dead (Hidden) Animal Betrays Self, 42, 48

72, Rabbit Rides Fox A-courting, 41–42, 45, 89

73, Blinding the Guard, 42, 45, 48

110, Belling the Cat, 49

122D, Let Me Catch You Better Game, 42, 48–49

126, The Sheep Chases the Wolf, 42

130, The Animals in Night Quarters, 40

155, The Ungrateful Serpent Returned to Captivity, 42

157, Learning to Fear Men, 90

175, The Tarbaby and the Rabbit, 43, 89

210, Cock, Duck, Hen, Pin, and Needle on a Journey, 40

291, Deceptive Tug-of-War, 40, 45

297A, Turtle's War Party, 40–41

653, The Four Skillful Brothers, 54–57, 63

653A, The Rarest Thing in the World, 54–59, 61–64, 87

653B, The Suitors Restore the Maiden to Life, 54, 56, 61–63

654, The Three Brothers, 49–50, 54–55

676, Open Sesame, 51

700, Tom Thumb, 51

759, God's Justice Vindicated, 39–40

945, Luck and Intelligence, 54, 63–64

1074, Race Won by Deception: Relative Helpers, 43, 89, 91

1530, Holding up the Rock, 42, 49

1641, Dr. Know-All, 90

1655, The Profitable Exchange, 49

1705, Talking Horse and Dog, 50

2053A, The House the Old Man Was to Build, 49

Note: Compilation of Tale Type and Motif references was done by Mary Navar, Bernard Timberg, and Edward Tittel.

[1]Tale Type numbers are taken from Antti Aarne and Stith Thompson, *The Types of the Folktale: A Classification and Bibliography,* FF Communications, no. 184, 2d rev. ed. (Helsinki, 1964).

AREWA TALE TYPES [2]

550, 44
1401, 47

LAMBRECHT TALE TYPES [3]

1462A, 47
1516, 49
1785, 49

THOMPSON MOTIF NUMBERS [4]

A163, Contests among the gods, 11–14
A164.3, Polygamy among the gods, 3–4, 7–9, 11–12
A284, God of thunder, 3, 5
A425.1, River goddess, 3
A934.11, River from transformation, 6–9, 12, 14
B210, The talking horse and dog, 50
B210.1, Person frightened by animals successively replying to his remarks, 50
B210.2, Talking animal or object refuses to talk on demand, 43, 50, 90
B211.1.7, Speaking dog, 50
B421, Helpful dog, 90
B524.1.2, Dogs rescue fleeing master from tree refuge, 45
C431, Tabu: uttering name of god (or gods), 7, 9
D1323, Magic object gives clairvoyance, 54–55, 63
D1323.15, Magic clairvoyant telescope, 54–55
D1335.1, Magic strength-giving food, 3
D1500.1.5.1, Magic healing apple, 54–55
D1520, Magic object affords miraculous transportation, 54–55, 63
D1520.19, Magic transportation by carpet, 54–55
E34, Resuscitation with misplaced head, 54, 56

---

[2]Erastus Ojo Arewa, "A Classification of the Folktales of the Northern East African Cattle Area by Types," Dissertation, University of California, Berkeley, 1966. Only those Arewa Tale Types not cross listed with Aarne-Thompson Tale Types are given here.

[3]Winifred Lambrecht, "A Tale Type Index for Central Africa," Dissertation, University of California, Berkeley, 1967. Only those Lambrecht Tale Types not cross listed with Aarne-Thompson Tale Types are given here.

[4]Motif numbers are taken from Stith Thompson, *Motif-Index of Folk-Literature*, 6 vols., rev. ed. (Bloomington, 1955–1958).

E106, Resuscitation by magic apple, 54–55
E125.1, Resuscitation by son, 54–55
F547.5, Extraordinary vagina, 11–12, 14
F547.6, Remarkable pubic hairs, 12, 14
F665.1, Skillful barber shaves running hare, 49
F715.2.5, River of tears, 6
H355.0.1, Who will find the most marvelous thing? 54–55
H500.1, Sons tested for skill, 55–56
H621, Skillful companions create woman: to whom does she belong? 54–56, 64
H621.1, Skillful companions resuscitate girl: to whom does she belong? 54–55
H621.2, Girl rescued by skillful companions: to whom does she belong? 55–56
H1154, Task: capturing animals, 37
H1154.6, Task: capturing squirrel and rattlesnake, 37–38
H1184, Task: cutting down tree without scratching for stinging insects, 47
J225, Choice: apparent injustice over greater wrong, 39–40
J1341.11, Hired men sing of displeasure with food; change song when food is improved, 90
J2413.4.2, Fowl makes another animal believe that he has had his neck cut off, 38
K22, Deceptive tug-of-war, 40
K263, Agreement not to scratch, 38, 47
K401.1, Dupe's food eaten and then blame fastened on him, 43–44
K543, Biting the foot, 48
K553.1, Let me catch you better game, 42, 48–49
K562.1, Captive trickster persuades captor to pray before eating, 44
K606, Escape by singing song, 45
K607.3, Sham-dead man deceived into making gesture, 48
K621, Escape by blinding the guard, 48
K622, Captive plays further and further from watchman and escapes, 45
K1000, Deception into self-injury, 3–4, 6–9, 13
K1055, Dupe persuaded to get into grass in order to learn new dance, 44
K1241, Trickster rides dupe horseback, 41–42
K1241.1, Trickster rides dupe a-courting, 41
K1500, Deception connected with adultery, 3
K1715, Weak animal (man) makes large one (ogre) believe that he has eaten many of the large one's companions, 49
K1723, Goat pretends to be chewing rock, 38, 47
K1800, Deception by disguise or illusion, 6–9
K1818, Disguise as a sick man, 41
K1956, Sham-wise man, 90
K2222, Treacherous co-wife (concubine), 3–4, 6–9, 13
M451.2, Death by drowning, 39
R111, Rescue of captive maiden, 55–56
S112.0.2, House burned with all inside, 39

S160.1, Self-mutilation, 3–5, 7–9, 13
S168, Mutilation: tearing off ears, 4, 10
S411, Wife banished, 7–8
T257.2, Jealousy of rival wives, 4, 6–7, 9
T271, The neglected wife, 4
W125, Gluttony, 5